Weaves and Pattern Drafting

John Tovey

VNR VAN NOSTRAND REINHOLD COMPANY
NEW YORK CINCINNATI TORONTO LONDON MELBOURNE

Acknowledgment

The Author wishes to thank those who have helped him in the preparation of this book, and in particular Miss Kathryn Cullen of C. S. Cullen (Photographers) Ltd.

Library of Congress Catalog Card Number 69–17675

ISBN 0–442–28565–5

Printed in Great Britain by litho at The Anchor Press Ltd
and bound by Wm Brendon & Son Ltd
both of Tiptree, Essex

Published in 1978 by Van Nostrand Reinhold Company
A division of Litton Educational Publishing, Inc.
135 West 50th Street, New York, NY 10020, U.S.A.

16 15 14 13 12 11 10 9 8 7 6 5 4 3 2 1

Contents

Bibliography

A Handweavers Pattern Book, M. Davison, Spencer International Press, New York

Advanced Textile Design, W. Watson, Longmans Green, London

Anni Albers on Designing, Wesleyan University Press, Middletown, Connecticut

Anni Albers on Weaving, Wesleyan University Press, Middletown, Connecticut

Byways in Handweaving, M. M. Atwater, Macmillan, London

Designing on the Loom, Mary Kirby, Studio, London

Domestic Manufactures Assistant, J. R. Bronson, Branford, Newton Centre, Massachusetts

Elementary Textile Design and Fabric Structure, John Read, Edward Arnold, London

Foot Power Loom Weaving, E. F. Worst, Bruce Publishing Co., Milwaukee, Wisconsin

Foundations of Fabric Structure, J. H. Strong, National Trade Press, London

Hand Loom Weaving, L. Hooper, Pitman, London

Hand Weaving Patterns from Finland, Pyysalo and Merisalo, Branford, Newton Centre, Massachusetts

How to Weave Linens, E. F. Worst, Bruce Publishing Co., Milwaukee, Wisconsin

Key to Weaving, M. Black, Spencer International Press, New York

Manual of Swedish Handweaving, Ulla Cyrus, Branford, Newton Centre, Massachusetts

Peter Collingwood: His Weaves and Weaving, Shuttlecraft of America, Monograph No 8

Shuttlecraft Book of American Handweaving, M. M. Atwater, Macmillan, London

Swedish Handweaving, Malin Selander, Studio, London

Textile Design and Colour, W. Watson, Longmans Green, London

Textile Terms and Definitions, The Textile Institute

The Technique of Rug Weaving, Peter Collingwood, Faber, London

The Weavers Book, Harriet Tidball, Macmillan, London

Treatise on the Art of Weaving, John Murphy, Blackie, London

Weaving Patterns, Malin Selander, Wezäta Forlag, Göteborg

Introduction

Throughout history man has always felt the need to decorate the things he made. As soon as the basic skills had been mastered some form of decoration appeared. Simple ornamentation grew quite naturally out of the materials being used and the techniques employed. Increasing skill and more sophisticated tools brought greater possibilities and, at the same time, the need for more discrimination. Typical examples are the sgraffito decoration on primitive pottery, twisting of square hand-forged wire in jewellery, the chevron pattern on the tablet-woven belts of the Pharaohs, and the tapered scrolls in wrought-iron work.

Woven textiles have developed considerably from the primitive fabrics as looms developed, particularly the draw loom. This led eventually to what is often considered to be the finest period of handweaving, the Italian work of the fourteenth and fifteenth centuries. Afterwards technique advanced more rapidly than design. With the invention of the Jacquard and the power loom greater facility for changing pattern and increased production led to the weaving of large quantities of particularly badly designed cloth. The draw loom, the finest example of a complex tool ever made, is now used by very few weavers, as its own complexity tends to limit its use, and the work is specialised. On the other hand the contemporary handweaver has a far greater range of materials and dyes to use than ever before, and what is perhaps more important, a much broader outlook. People are far less content to copy what has already been done, and are more concerned about expressing their own ideas. Though the obvious field for this type of work is the individually woven wall decoration or rug, there is considerable scope for design in dress and furnishing textiles. It is with this in mind that this book has been written.

(i) Factors in design

The design of woven fabric depends on three things, colour, pattern and texture. Colour can be inherent in the materials employed, or can be dyed. Texture is partly that of the material and partly the texture of the weave. The simplest and often the most effective texture results from the use of fancy yarns, or yarns of different thicknesses in a plain weave or variations of this (see chapter 1). This gives tremendous scope for experiment, even on the simplest looms, but with a four-shaft loom this can be developed further by using weaves which themselves have interesting texture, such as honeycomb, mock leno, the twills and the satins.

Pattern is used here in the limited sense of decoration produced with an extra set of threads in addition to the basic cloth, e.g. traditional overshot patterns; or a more complex cloth structure, e.g. double cloth or damask.

To these can be added the range of patterns produced by combining simple weaves with additional colour in both warp and weft, giving checks and tartans and all the colour and weave effects (see chapter 10).

Colour is a very personal thing, and although much has been written on the theory of colour, in the end it is the weaver's decision. A simple but arbitrary division of colours is into two groups, the natural and the man-made. The natural range would include both the colours of the materials, e.g. sea-grass, rushes, raffia, moorit Shetland and Black Welsh fleeces, Maltese cotton, tussah and Shantung silks, and the colours of an allied range like the earth colours of yellow ochre and Indian red, and the majority of colours obtained from natural dyestuffs. In contrast to these the man-made colours are the strong pure colours of the new dyes, powerful enough to remain constant on almost any materials, therefore giving more scope for design, but needing far more skill and artistry in their use. The natural colours are relatively easy to use, but the synthetics are vastly more exciting, as even a brief examination of modern tapestries and rugs will show.

The texture of materials can be similarly divided, with cellophane, nylon, perspex, etc. taking the place of the man-made dyes, and having likewise, a wide scope but needing more careful handling.

The texture of the weave has to be considered from two points of view, the artistic and the technical designs of cloth. For brevity the artistic design will be referred to as 'design', and the technical design as 'structure'. Design is considered in relation to colour schemes, styles, lighting, furniture, etc. Structure includes function, handle, weight, durability, finish and cost. The choice of structural texture may be influenced considerably by the way that the colour is to be used, and the scale of the texture and the appearance of the cloth are affected by both design and structure.

Pattern is possibly the greatest single factor which attracts people to handweaving. There is a fascination in watching a pattern develop pick by pick as the cloth is woven, and this is even greater if the pattern is designed by the weaver. It may be small in scale or so large that the repeat is the whole width of the loom, a simple overshot or a twenty-shaft double weave with a compound mounting, but whatever it is, it should be an expression of the craftsman's personality and not a lifeless reproduction of another weaver's work. Old work can be copied to discover the techniques used, and the knowledge gained should be used to create new fabrics in keeping with contemporary living while maintaining the tradition of imaginative and original work.

(ii) Reading and writing drafts and weave plans

In woven cloth there are two sets of threads at right angles to each other, the warp threads or ends running the length of the cloth, and the weft threads or picks running across the width. The mechanism of the loom divides the warp into two layers, between which the shuttle carries the pick of weft. The order of interlacing the warp and weft can be represented on paper in two ways, either by a diagrammatic representation of the cloth itself, which is known as the 'weave plan', or by giving the order of threading the loom and of lifting the shafts. Both are often combined in one diagram, although either by itself is sufficient. The ways of representing the threading and lifting plan are many and varied, but for the weave plan squared or point paper is a necessity.

The warp ends are represented by the spaces between the vertical lines (*1*), and the picks of weft by the spaces between the horizontal lines (*2*).

1 Warp threads

2 Weft threads

Where any one end crosses a pick one or other must be on the face of the cloth in the common single-layer cloth of only one warp and weft (*3*). (In cloths with two warps or wefts, or both, this does not necessarily occur.)

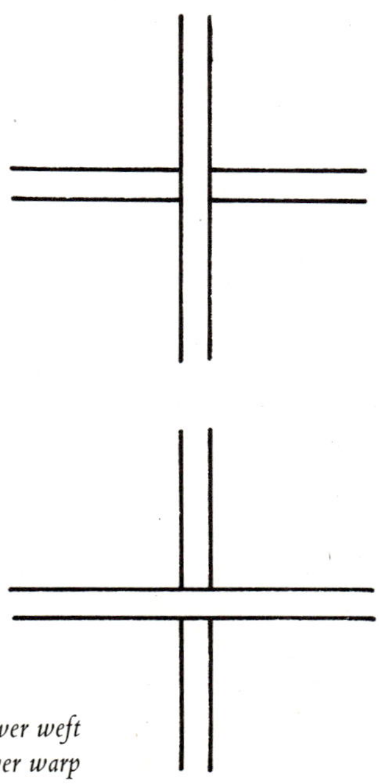

3 (a) Warp over weft
(b) Weft over warp

Each small square therefore shows a crossing of warp over weft or vice versa. If one set of threads is now assumed to be black, the squares representing any of these threads on top must now be blacked in or given some other distinguishing mark (*4*).

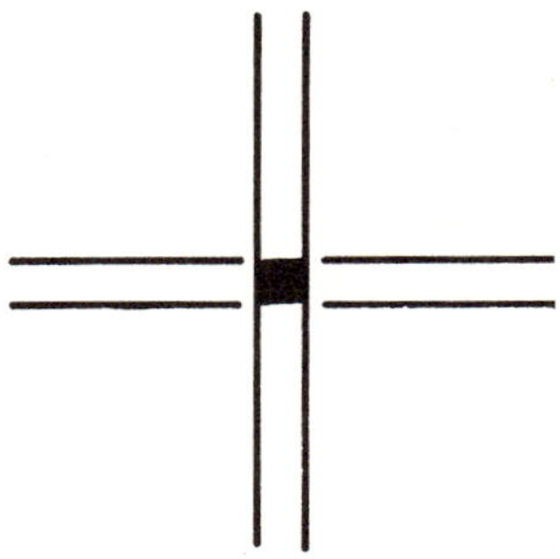

4 Warp over weft, marks to rise (counter-march)

Although either set can be indicated it is more usual to find the rising warp ends marked, as they are easier to distinguish on the loom than either the sinking ends or the weft, and are therefore more easily visualised. In a weave plan for a counter-balanced loom in which the sinking shed is tied to the lamms, marking the sinking warp ends may be easier (*5*).

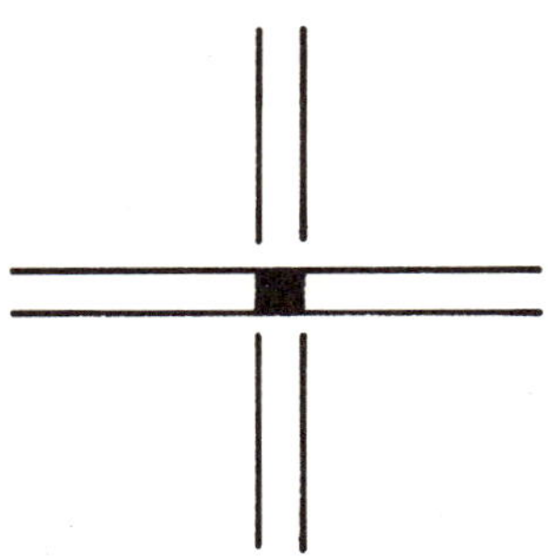

5 Weft over warp, marks to fall (counter-balanced)

As the warp is controlled directly by the loom it is always easier to think of the warp rising or falling than the weft going under or over, except for weaves like the traditional overshot patterns in which the pattern weft is obviously the main factor. Unless they are indicated 'marks to fall', all weave plans may be read as 'marks to rise', the warp being referred to in each case.

The connection between the weave plan and the cloth is easily demonstrated by weaving a sample using a black warp and white weft. The resulting cloth will correspond to a weave plan with rising warp marks (*6*).

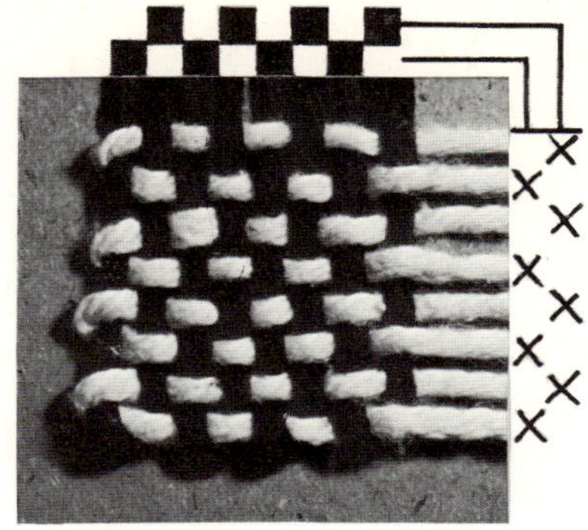

6 Cloth with threading and lifting (marks to rise)

(*7*) The corresponding weave plan.

7 Weave plan of plain weave

The threading draft is a simplified view of the shafts from above. The warp ends are represented by the vertical columns as before, and run up above the weave plan (*8*).

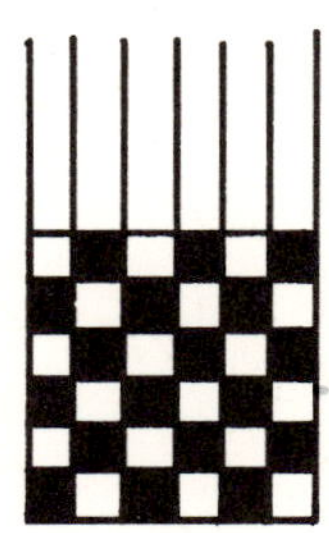

8 Weave plan with warp threads extended upwards

The horizontal rows now represent the shafts (*9*).

9 Weave plan with shafts added

Each small square now indicates a warp end crossing a shaft (*10*).

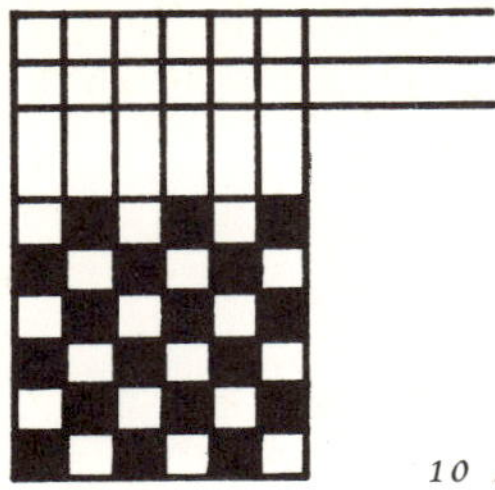

10 Ends crossing shafts

A heddle on a shaft would appear as a straight line on the loom itself (*11*).

11 Heddles on shafts

Each warp end crosses both shafts, but can be threaded through only one heddle, which would appear above it, and is represented by filling in the square above it. The complete threading draft will now appear like this (*12*).

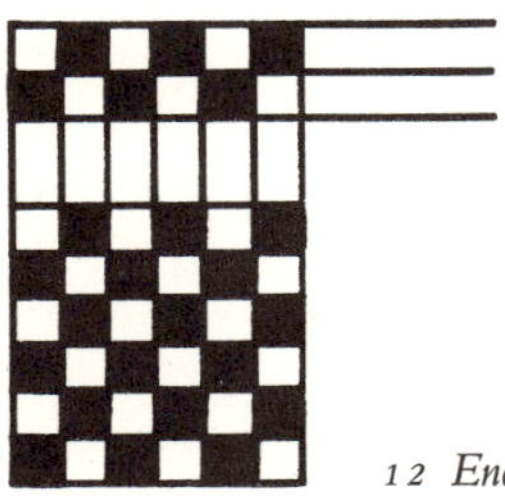

12 Ends marked on shafts

The lifting plan can be developed weft way from the weave plan as the threading draft was developed warp way. The horizontal lines of weft can be extended sideways (*13*).

13 Weave plan with weft threads extended sideways

The lines of the shafts are brought down the side to cross over them (*14*).

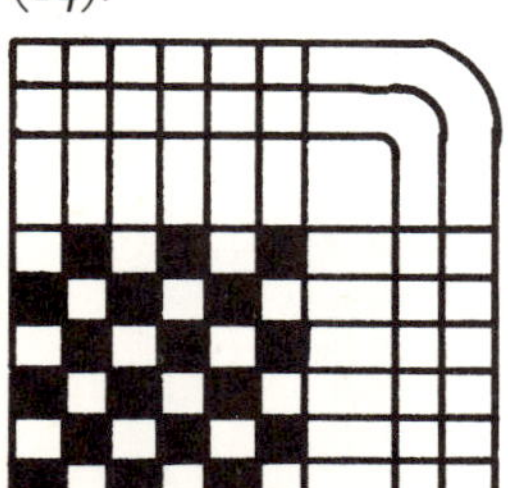

14 Shafts bent down

The shaft which has to be lifted for any row is marked where it crosses that row (*15*).

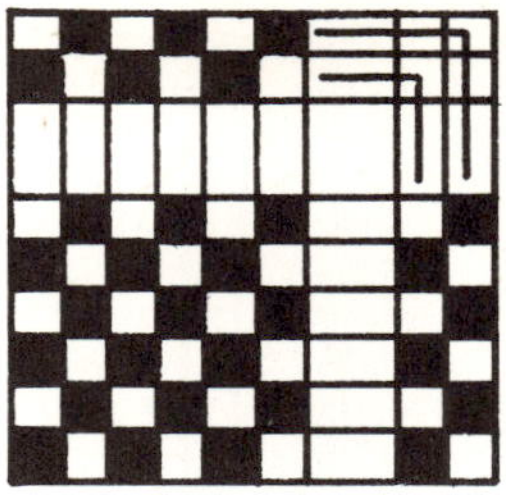

15 Lifting plan added

This gives the complete plan as it is usually drawn.

The plan for the foot power loom is basically the same, the lifting plan being replaced by the tie-up and treadling draft. The vertical columns to the right of the weave plan now represent the treadles, and are extended upwards to cross the shafts (*16*).

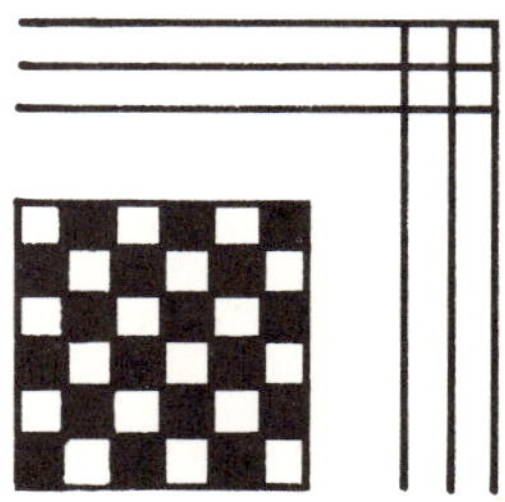

16 Treadles added to shafts

The small squares represent the possible connections between shafts and treadles, and the shaft operated by either treadle is marked by filling in the square on the treadle in line with the shaft (*17a, b*).

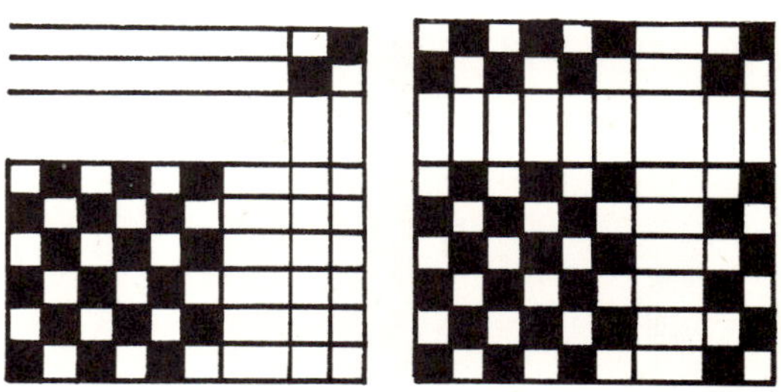

17 (a) Treadles tied to shafts
(b) Full weave diagram (i.e. weave plan with threading draft and either lifting plan or tie-up and treadling plan)

In the diagram treadle (A) operates shaft 1, and treadle (B) operates shaft 2. Threading on four shafts saves crowding the heddles on the shafts (*18*).

The threading is a straight draft, shaftes 1 and 3 working together and replacing shaft 1 in the two-shaft draft, and controlling all the odd threads, shafts 2 and 4 likewise replacing shaft 2. The lifting plan now has to cover four shafts (*a*). This is written as a treadling plan for a foot power loom (*b*). It is shown in the four-shaft plain weave (*18*). The only complication is that on the counter-balanced loom the tie-up is a sinking tie. This means that either the fabric is woven face downwards, or the blanks and marks have to be transposed.

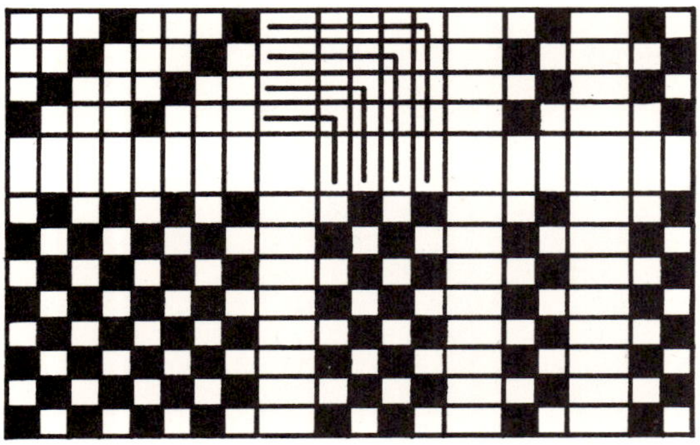

18 Weave plan with draft and lifting plan; tie-up and treadling plans for both rising and sinking shed

(iii) Planning treadling drafts

One of the main advantages of a foot power loom is that each shed usually requires only one treadle, which operates all the shafts necessary for that shed. The resulting increase in speed directly affects the quality of the cloth, as the weaving can be steady and rhythmic, with the picks at a consistent tension laid evenly in the cloth. The smoothest working is obtained when treadling is done with alternate feet, and all treadling plans should be arranged with this in mind, even if it means occasionally tying the same combination of shafts on to two different treadles. The tie-up and lifting plans given in most books are drafted for clarity of understanding the weave, and it is left to the individual weaver to rearrange them to suit himself. Examples of practical arrangements follow in diagrams *19* to *23*.

(*19a–c*) The four-shaft straight twill theoretical tie-up (*a*) becomes (*b*). This used to be written as (*c*) to save space when the weave plan was not required, the order of treadling being given by the numbers in the columns for the treadles.

19 (a) Theoretical tie-up for $\frac{2}{2}$ twill
(b) Practical tie-up for $\frac{2}{2}$ twill using graphic draft for treadling plan
(c) Practical tie-up for $\frac{2}{2}$ twill using numbers for treadling plan

(*20a–d*) The theoretical and practical tie-ups are the same in a traditional overshot weave, as the pattern and plain wefts alternate. One foot remains on the pattern treadle for the block being woven, the other works heel and toe on the plain weave treadles. These are usually the right-hand pair as they are lighter to use (being further from the pivot of the marches), and most people are right-footed as well as right-handed (*a*).

The same principle applies in the spot weaves with one plain shaft and several spotting shafts, or several spotting shafts and a ground shaft (*b*).

The very small Bronson (spot) weave (which is also a mock leno), uses three treadles in the same way (*c*).

The same weave with alternate warp- and weft-faced blocks is treadled as (*d*). This order of treadling is frequently used in the mock leno and huckaback groups. Plain weave is on the centre two shafts.

This method of writing the threading draft in short strokes instead of squares is more concise for long drafts, and as it does not need point paper it is ideal for notes in a record book. The graphic version of the treadling draft is more compact than on point paper, and is more legible as a visual pattern than the numbers used in diagrams *21* to *23*, which are the most concise of all.

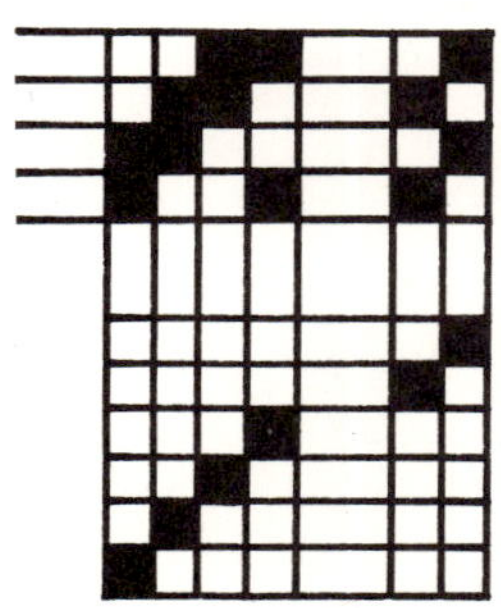

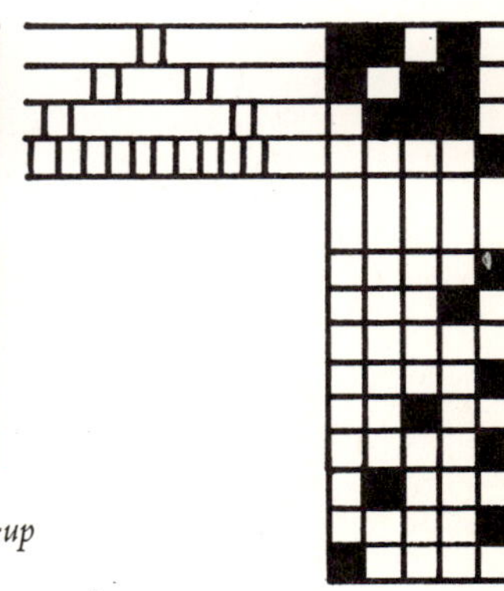

20 (a) Overshot weave tie-up
(b) Spot weave tie-up

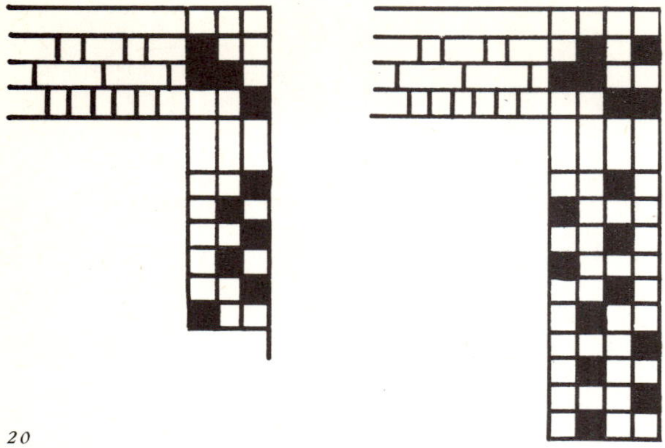

20
(c) Mock leno weave tie-up *(d) Canvas weave tie-up*

(*21a, b*) Honeycomb has an odd number of treadles (*a*), but as the treadling draft is a point this presents no problem (*b*).

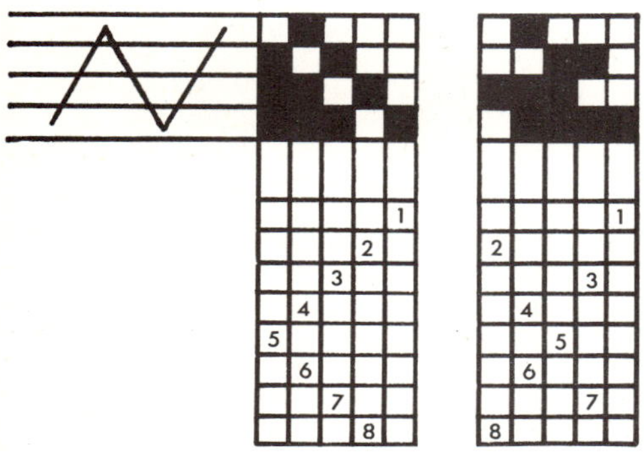

21 *(a) Honeycomb tie-up, theoretical*
(b) Honeycomb tie-up, practical

(*22a, b*) A three-shaft twill is difficult to treadle logically on three treadles, but when it is drafted on five treadles (two duplicates and one used twice), they can be worked over toe and heel with alternate feet (*a*).

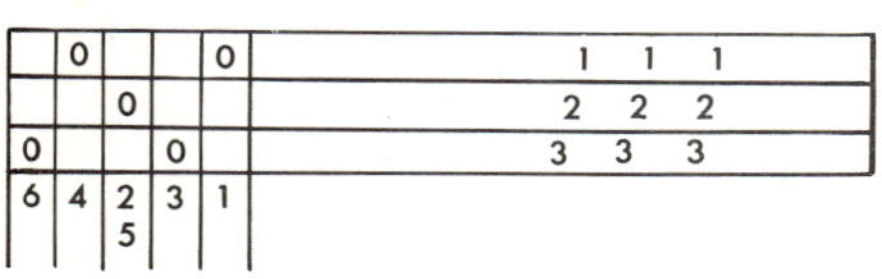

22 *(a) Three-shaft (or three-end) twill (redrawn from John Murphy's* Treatise*)*

The same principle is applied to a five-end twill, with three treadles duplicated and two used twice (*b*).

'The five leafed tweel in sometimes woven with one foot, and sometimes with both, though only five treadles are employed; to make the treading of the feet alternate without interruption, eight treadles are necessary, as under.'

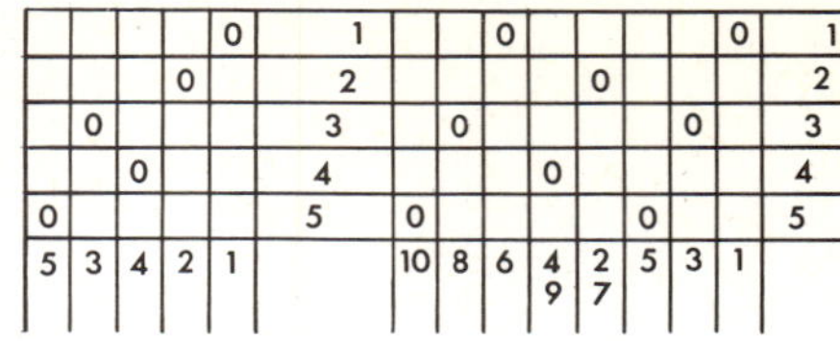

22 *(b) Five-end twill (redrawn from John Murphy's* Treatise*)*

(*23a, b*) Eight-shaft twills present a problem as the stretch across the treadles can be uncomfortably wide, (*a*) is a good arrangement as the treadling is symmetrical and the weaver remains balanced in the centre of the loom; (*b*) is another draft, which requires less stretch, but can lead to beating off-centre as the feet work across the loom.

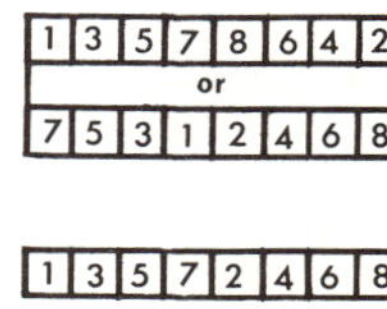

23a, b Eight-end twill, alternative orders of treadling

(iv) Abbreviations

As well as the rapid forms of draft writing used above (*19c–22*), several other abbreviations are useful (*24–28*).

(*24a–d*) In the threading drafts for spot weaves with a plain shaft the ends need not be indicated on it as it must carry alternate ends all through the draft.

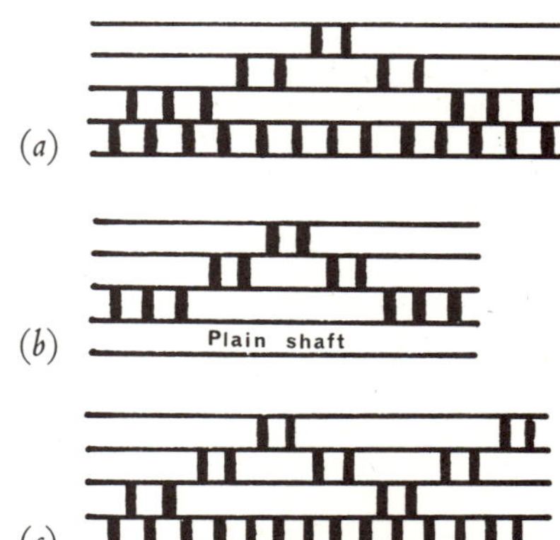

24 *Spot drafts abbreviated*
(a) Spot draft with ground shaft and two spotting shafts
(b) Spot draft with ground shaft and two spotting shafts
(c) Spot draft with three spotting shafts

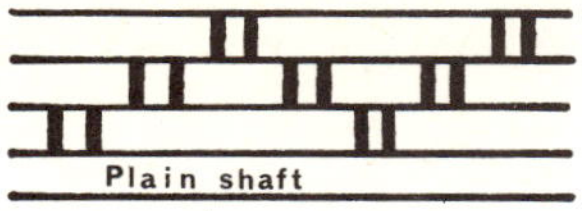

(d) Spot draft with three spotting shafts

(*25a–g*) Twills, double weave, damask drafts and any others based on straight runs and not blocks can be written as straight lines. (*a*) is a four-shaft straight draft written obliquely or vertically, (*b*) and (*c*) are waved or point drafts on four shafts, (*c*) having the turning-point on shaft 1 each time. (*d*) is a draft which can be used for double weave, double-faced twill, or damask. (*e–g*) shows a variety of eight-shaft twills, doubled straight, point, doubled point.

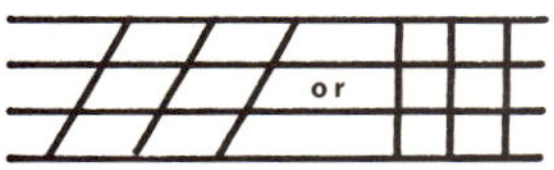

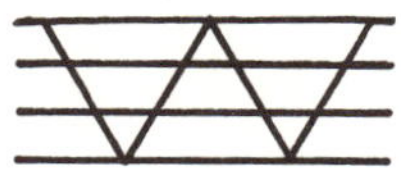

25 *Abbreviated form of drafts*
(a) Four-shaft straight draft
(b) Four-shaft point or waved draft, six end

(c) Four-shaft point or waved draft, eight end

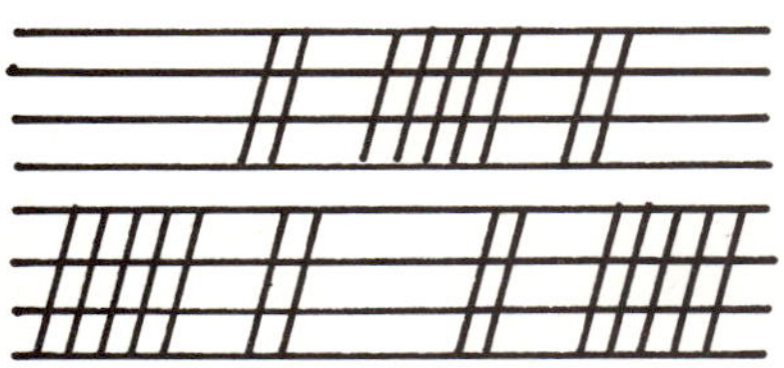

(d) Eight-shaft two-block draft

(e) Eight-shaft doubled straight draft

(f) Eight-shaft point draft

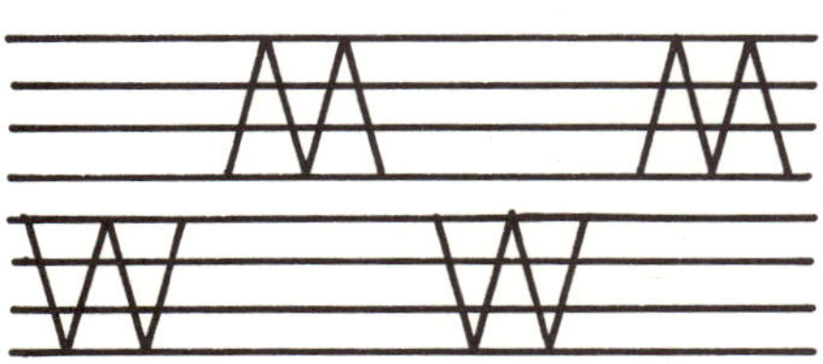

(g) Eight-shaft doubled point draft

(*26*) Weaves of the mock leno and huckaback groups are drafted 'M and W'.

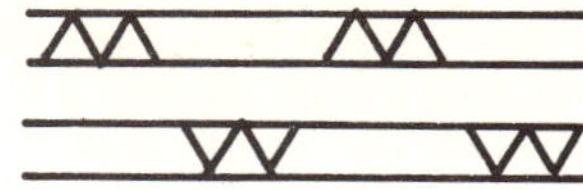

26 *Abbreviated huckaback and canvas weave draft*

(*27a–c*) When stating a weave, particularly regular twill weaves or twill-based weaves, the number of warp ends rising and falling is written as an extended fraction, (*a*) is a plain weave, one end raised and one sunk, (*b*) a two up and two down twill, and (*c*) an eight-shaft twill. The cross-sections are through the warp, and if the weft is imagined stretched until it is straight, the number of ends above and below are the numerals of the fractions.

27 *Numbering of the order of lifting of weaves*
(a) Plain weave
(b) Two up two down twill (four end)
(c) 3, 2, 1, 2 twill (eight end)

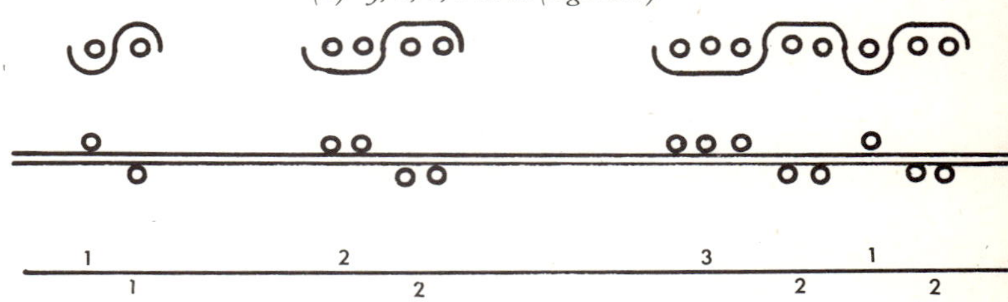

(*28a–c*) In weaves on a straight draft running upwards to the right the normal lifting plan will be the same as one repeat of the weave. (*a*) shows one repeat of a twill. In any draft with a section of threads running upwards to the right across all the shafts, the weave plan on these ends will be the lifting plan. In the honeycomb in (*b*) the weave plan of the first four ends is the lifting plan, and in the 5 × 5 mock leno in (*c*) the weave plan of the centre four ends is the lifting plan. The term 'woven as drawn in' applied to the traditional overshot weaves means that each block of the draft in order is woven square, working from the right-hand selvedge.

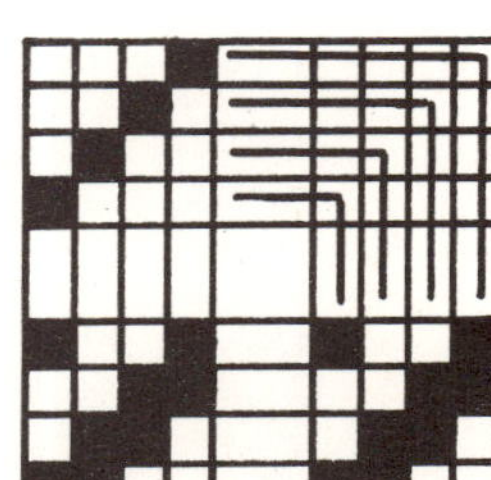

28 *Lifting plan as weave plan*
(a) Four-end twill, four-shaft straight draft

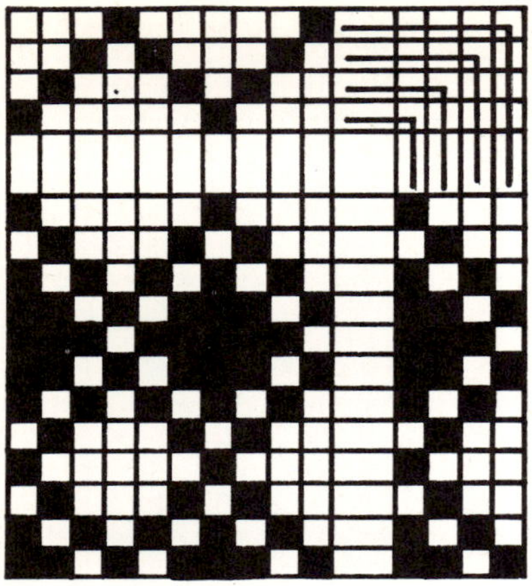

28 (b) *Four-end honeycomb, four-shaft waved draft*

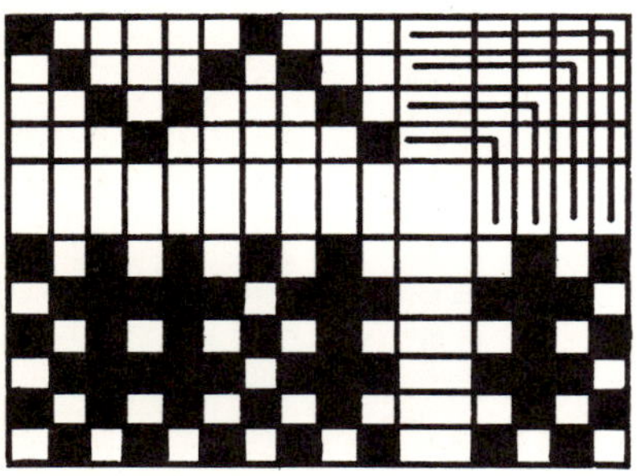

28 (c) *5 × 1 mock leno, four-shaft waved draft*

(v) Writing drafts from a weave plan

(*29a–f*) Working out the threading and lifting from a given weave plan is quite easy if it is done methodically. The ends are taken in turn from left to right, and each end which works differently is given a different shaft. In (*a*) the first end works plain, starting over the first pick, and is given shaft 1 (*b*). The second end works three down, three up, and is placed on shaft 2 (*c*). The third end works the same as the first, so is placed on shaft 1 (*d*). The second half is done in the same way. Ends four and six work plain, but start *under* the first pick so they are given shaft 3, and end five works three up three down (the reverse of end two), and has shaft 4 (*e*). If shafts 1 and 2 are transposed the familiar point draft emerges, and with the straight draft appearing in the centre (ends two, three, four and five), the lifting plan is as the weave plan.

29 *Development of threading and lifting from the weave plan*
(*a*) *Weave plan (small canvas weave)*
(*b*) *Placing the first end on the threading draft*
(*c*) *Placing the second end on the threading draft*
(*d*) *Placing the third end on the threading draft*
(*e*) *Placing the second group of ends*
(*f*) *Rearranging into the standard form and completing the weave diagram*

1 Plain weave and its derivatives

The simplest weave of all is the plain weave or tabby, in which the ends work one up and one down, and the picks run under one over one. It can vary from a hard stiff cloth like sail cloth to a fine semi-transparent organdie. It has the maximum number of interlacings per repeat of the weave, each pair of threads from either warp or weft being separated by a thread from the opposite set. This means that for yarns of a given count fewer threads can be woven into a plain cloth than cloths in which ends or picks float over two or more threads, i.e. a cloth that would take sixteen ends per inch in plain weave could take twenty to twenty-two ends per inch in a 2 and 2 hopsack or 2 and 2 twill.

The structure is firm and inclined to be stiff. The surface is uniform and free of floats which could be accidentally caught.

Although it is structurally the simplest weave of all, it has greater inherent possibilities for design than any other single weave. With the same thickness of warp and weft the fabric could be plain, have sections of warp spaced widely and closely alternately, have groups of ends alternating with spaces in the reed, and the same variations can be made in the weft. Different thicknesses of warp and weft will, with the correct sett, produce warp-faced or weft-faced cloths, warp and weft ribs; and thick and thin threads in both warp and weft will give a repp.

(i) Plain weave threading

(i) *a* *Balanced* (*30*) Plain weave is usually woven on two or four shafts, two for coarse warps or warps with an open sett, and four if the warp is fine or inclined to fluff as it saves crowding the heddles on the shafts and so increasing the difficulties. The usual draft is straight, with a lift of 1 and 3, then 2 and 4 (*31a*). The old weavers used a sateen draft with a lift of 1 and 2, then 3 and 4 (*31b*).

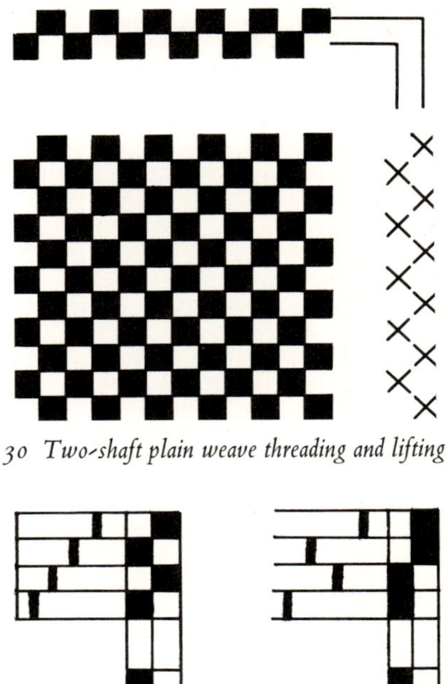

30 Two-shaft plain weave threading and lifting

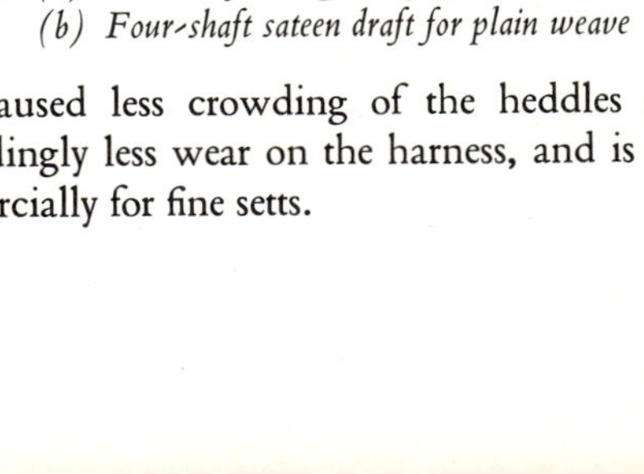

31 (a) Four-shaft straight draft for plain weave
(b) Four-shaft sateen draft for plain weave

This caused less crowding of the heddles and correspondingly less wear on the harness, and is still used commercially for fine setts.

(i) *b* *Weft rib* (*32a*, *b*) Ribs are produced in plain weave by unbalancing the structure. A more widely spaced warp (roughly half of the normal square sett), will allow the weft to beat up more and so cover the warp, giving weft ribs running the length of the cloth (*a*). (A weft-faced rib runs warp way, as the weft covers the warp ends and makes a flattened tube of weft round the warp.) The rib can be accentuated either by using a coarse warp and fine weft, or by extending the plain weave horizontally, i.e. letting several ends work as one (*33*).

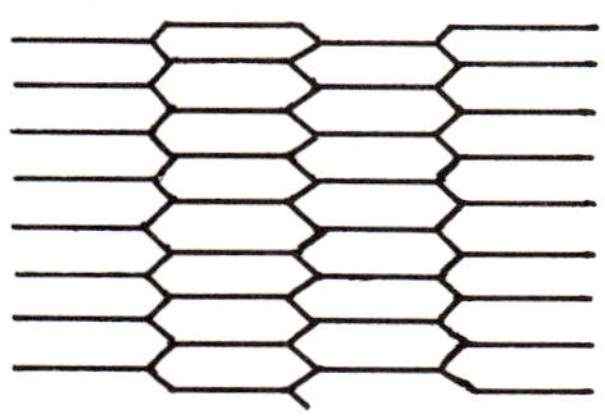

32 Weft-faced rib

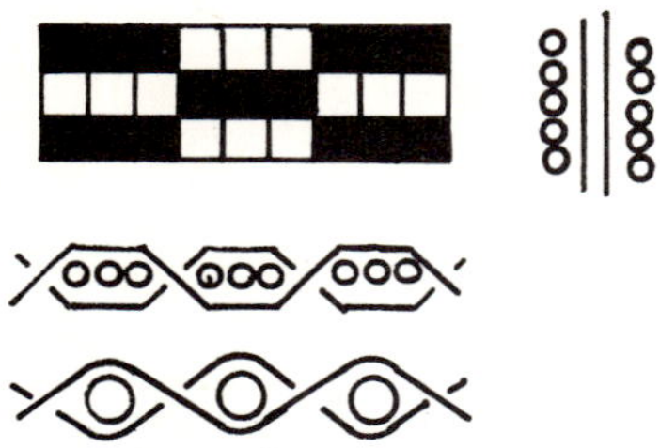

33 Plain weave extended horizontally (weft rib)

(i) *c* *Warp rib* A warp rib running across the fabric is produced by transposing the conditions, using a fine close warp and a coarse weft (*34*), or extending the plain weave vertically and weaving several picks as one (*35*).

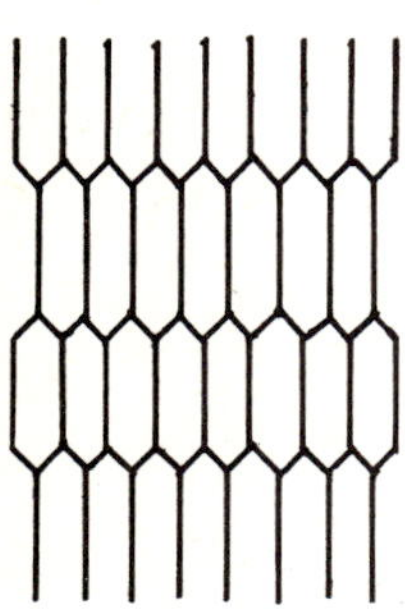

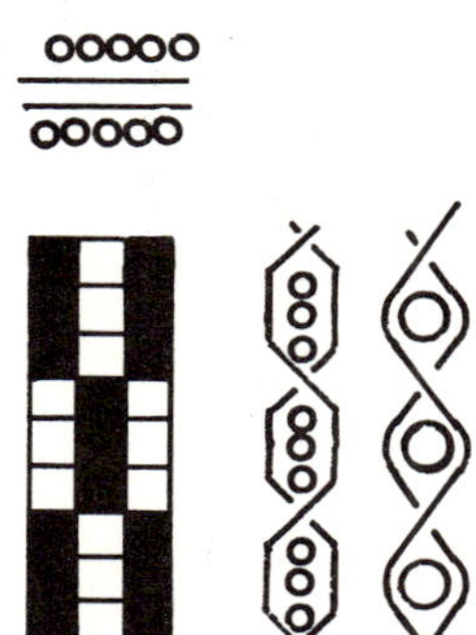

34 Warp-faced rib

35 Plain weave extended vertically (warp rib)

(i) *d* *Repp* A repp has alternately ends and picks of fine and coarse yarns, the coarse ends being raised over the coarse picks. The effect is improved by weaving with the fine warp at a greater tension, using two warp rollers (*36*).

36 Cross-section of repp

(ii) Plain weave derivatives

(ii) *a* *Hopsack* (*37a*, *b*) The hopsack weave is a plain weave extended warp way and weft way. It is commonly used with two ends and picks working as one for tweeds. It can be woven on two shafts by doubling the threads in the heddles, or better still, by using two separate heddles. In each case the warp should be reeded with two ends per dent, the reed wire coming between the ends working the same to prevent twisting. The weft can be doubled in the shuttle, or two shuttles used, or catching ends placed on one side.

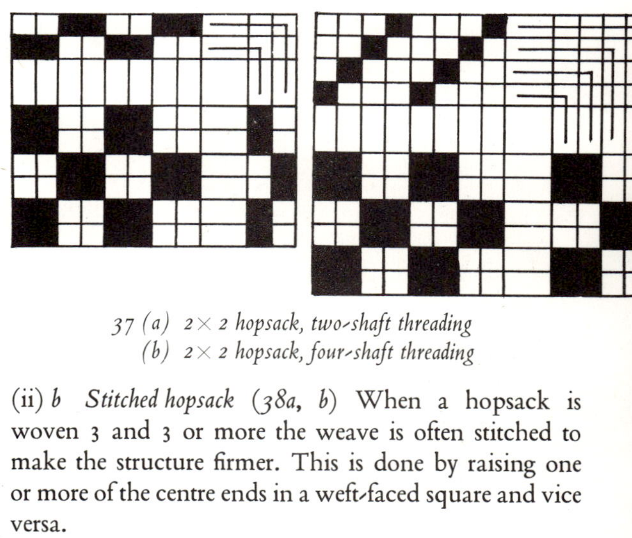

37 (a) 2×2 hopsack, two-shaft threading
(b) 2×2 hopsack, four-shaft threading

(ii) *b* *Stitched hopsack* (*38a*, *b*) When a hopsack is woven 3 and 3 or more the weave is often stitched to make the structure firmer. This is done by raising one or more of the centre ends in a weft-faced square and vice versa.

38 (a) 3×3 plain hopsack

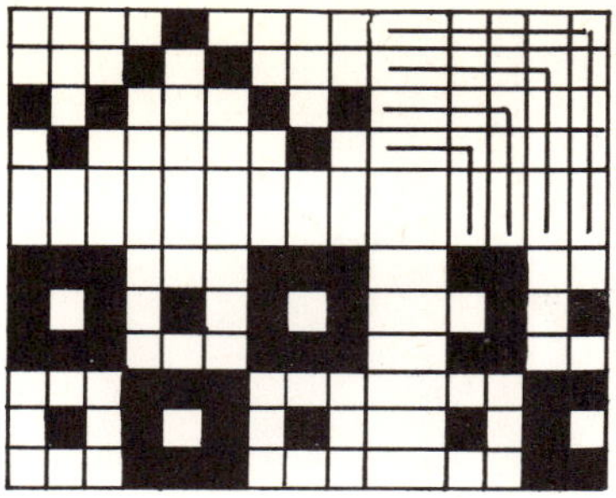

(b) 3 × 3 stitched hopsack

(ii) *c Hopsack derivatives* (*39*) Hopsack weave is often combined with warp and weft ribs for added firmness and surface interest. The ends and picks making the warp and weft ribs can be woven in finer yarns.

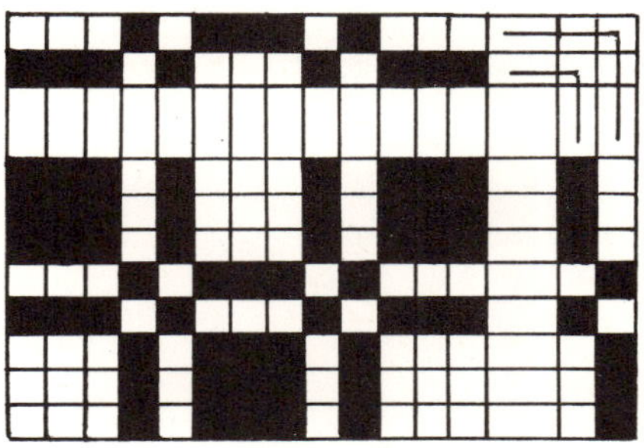

39 Hopsack with rib

(*40*) A twilled hopsack can be woven on eight shafts with a straight draft, and lifting as weave plan.

40 Eight-end twilled hopsack or Barathea weave

(*41*) Barley-corn is a hopsack combined with a twill and also needs an eight-shaft draft, lifting as weave plan.

41 Barley-corn (lifting plan as weave plan)

2 Twills

A plain twill is a diagonal weave in which the threads float over two or more threads of the opposite set, and the float moves one thread sideways on each successive pick. It can be woven on any number of ends from three upwards.

The twill cloth is more pliable than a plain weave, and has more diagonal stretch, which makes it more suitable for tailored garments. With yarns of the same count it is heavier than a plain weave as there are fewer intersections in the weave, and the threads can lie closer together in the cloth (*42*).

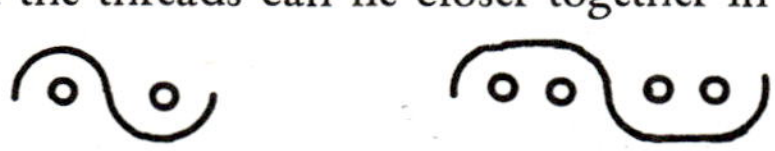

42 Cross-section of plain weave and twill

The twist of the yarns has an effect on the twill line. If warp and weft are of the same twist (either both S twist or both Z twist), the fibres on the back of the top thread lie at the same angle as those on the top of the back thread, and tend to bed in in the finishing and conceal the weave (*43*).

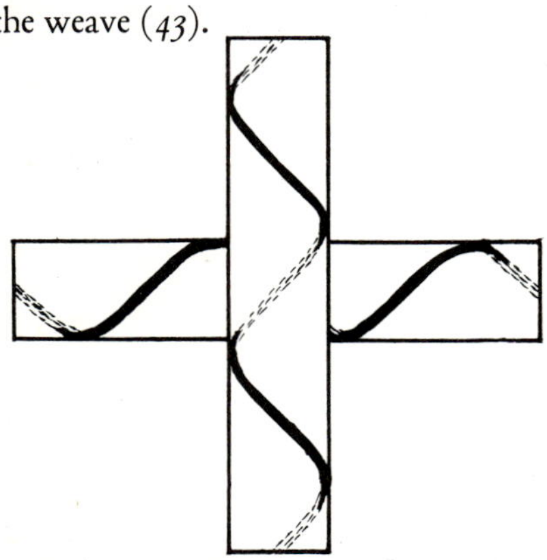

43 Two S-twist yarns crossing

If warp and weft are of opposite twist the surface fibres of the yarns where they touch are now at right angles, and stand off and show the weave (*44*).

44 One S- and one Z-twist yarns crossing

If the twill line opposes the run of the surface fibres it is more clearly defined, but a twill running with the fibres is subdued. For this reason a herringbone weave shows alternately clear and indefinite stripes.

Types of twill are known by name in industry, and several have become household words. A Jean twill is a 2 and 1 warp- or weft-faced weave, and in cotton is used for overalls. A drill is a warp-faced 2 and 1, 3 and 1 or 4 and 1 twill weave, with the twill running against the twist of the yarn, and is used for uniform cotton cloth.

(i) Plain twills

(i) *a* *Three shaft* (*45*) This is the smallest number of shafts on which a twill can be woven, and gives a warp-

or weft-faced twill. With about 50 per cent more ends than picks per inch in a warp face it gives a gabardine structure. It is a weave which deserves to be used more by handweavers than it is. The difficulty of cording a three-shaft counter-balanced harness with pulleys or rollers can easily be overcome if the special mounting is used. (See *The Technique of Weaving*, page 23, diagram 31.)

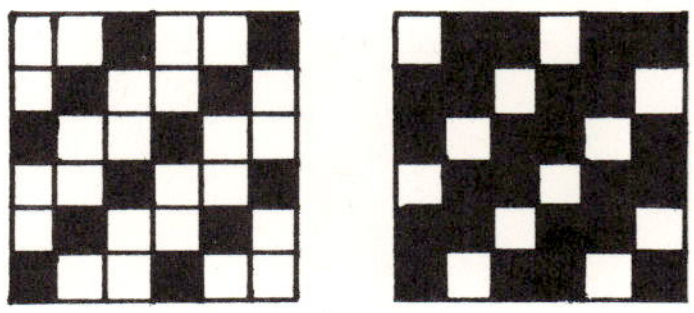

45 *(a) Three-end twill, weft face*
(b) Three-end twill, warp face (lifting as weave plan)

(i) *b* *Four shaft* (*46*) With four shafts, three types of twill can be woven, a balanced $\frac{2}{2}$ (*a*), a warp-faced $\frac{3}{1}$ (*b*), and a weft-faced $\frac{1}{3}$ (*c*). The balanced twill is woven square, while the warp-faced twill is not. (See section (ii) *a*.)

46 *(a) Balanced four-shaft twill*
(b) Warp-faced four-shaft twill
(c) Weft-faced four-shaft twill

Variations of plain twills (*51*).

Variations are produced by reversing the angle of the twill in threading or lifting, or both. Reversing either one or the other reverses the twill line, reversing both leaves it unchanged. This is employed to make waves (ii)*a*, diamonds (ii)*b*, herringbone (iii)*a*, weft-way herringbone (i)*c*, and, on a small scale, a broken twill (iv) *a*, and a small barley-corn (*47*).

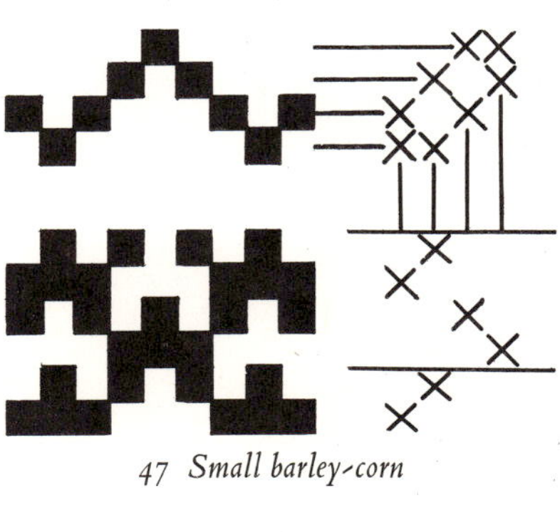

47 *Small barley-corn*

(i) *c* *Five shaft* (*48a, b*) Five is the smallest number of shafts on which a true satin (see chapter 3) can be woven. It is also the smallest number on which a weave of two sections can be woven, i.e. a fine twill on a plain weave ground (*b*). Apart from this the weave is not of much interest.

48 *Five-end twill*
(a) Weave plan
(b) Cross-section

(i) *c* *Eight shaft* (*49*) An eight-shaft twill can be of two, four or six parts. Two parts, from $\frac{1}{7}$ to $\frac{7}{1}$ give two lines of differing widths, and as the number of ends is high (8) compared with the number of intersections (2), the weave is loose and can take a comparatively high sett. Six parts on eight shafts gives fine lines on a plain weave ground, e.g. $\frac{1\,1\,2}{1\,1\,2}$, $\frac{1\,2\,1}{1\,1\,2}$, $\frac{2\,2\,1}{1\,1\,1}$ and $\frac{3\,1\,1}{1\,1\,1}$, which is a useful upholstery weave (*50c*). As the ratio of ends to intersections is now low, 8 to 6, the cloth is firm and need not be set too closely.

(a) $\frac{1}{7}$ *(b)* $\frac{4}{4}$

49 *Cross-sections of eight-end twills*

Four parts give the greatest variety, $\frac{3\,1}{2\,2}$, $\frac{3\,1}{3\,1}$, $\frac{4\,2}{1\,1}$, etc. giving warp or weft lines of differing widths. The ends to intersections ratio is good, 8 to 4, so the cloth is quite firm but supple. The weave plan (*49a, b*) shows the $\frac{3\,1}{2\,2}$ and $\frac{3\,1}{3\,1}$ twills, and (*52a, b, c*) shows a cotton cloth with these two and the $\frac{3\,1\,1}{1\,1\,1}$ twill.

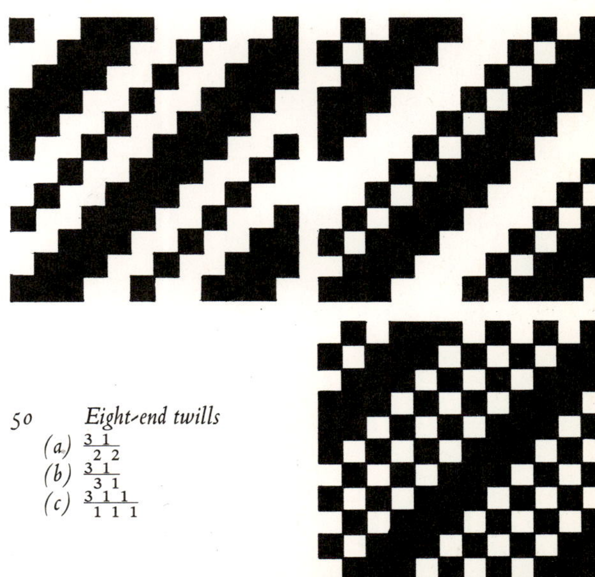

50 *Eight-end twills*
(a) $\frac{3\,1}{2\,2}$
(b) $\frac{3\,1}{3\,1}$
(c) $\frac{3\,1\,1}{1\,1\,1}$

51 *Variations of plain twills*

52 *Eight-end twills*
(*a*) $\frac{3\ 1}{3\ 1}$
(*b*) $\frac{3\ 1}{2\ 2}$
(*c*) $\frac{3\ 1\ 1}{1\ 1\ 1}$

With eight shafts many different threadings are possible. As well as the usual straight, point, waved, zigzag drafts, doubled straight, doubled and trebled wave, etc. give good and interesting weaves (53).

53 *Eight-end twills, variations of drafting*

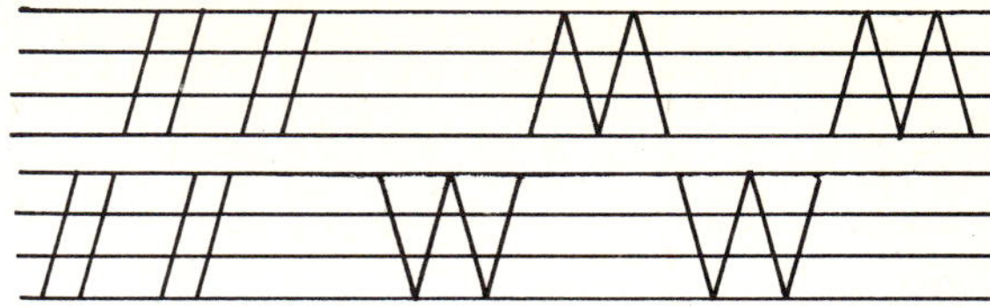

Adding more shafts beyond eight merely increases the capacity for detail without affecting the general principles.

(ii) Modified twills

The plain 45° twill can be altered in several ways, most of which result in the angle being raised or lowered, as well as in a change in the character of the cloth.

(ii) *a* *High-angle or steep twills* (*54a–c*) The simplest way of producing a high twill is to use a finer more closely set warp, a 2 and 2 twill woven in this way giving a gabardine.

54 *Rearranged twills*
(*a*) *Five-end whipcord or Venetian twill*
(*b*) *Four-end eight-pick fine whipcord*
(*c*) *Seven-end seven-pick whipcord*

Another way is to rearrange the existing twills by taking half the ends of a twill which repeats on an even number of ends, or alternate ends of a twill with an odd number of ends. (*a*) is a five end five pick Venetian or fine whipcord taking every other end, and as the weave is on an odd number of ends every end is used. (*b*) shows a four end eight pick fine whipcord which, following the same plan, results in only the odd ends being used. (*c*) is a 7 end 7 pick whipcord using alternate ends. In steep twills the warp should predominate.

(ii) *b* *Low-angle or flat twills* These are constructed from the relevant plain twills in a similar way by using the picks instead of the ends, and should be weft faced. In this case the marks should indicate weft up instead of the more usual warp.

(ii) *c* *Combination twills* These are formed by drafting a small twill weave on the odd ends of the combination weave, and a second small twill on the even ends, thus giving a flat twill; or drafting on picks to give a steep twill. A useful crêpe weave which is not strictly a combination twill is formed by combining a 2 and 2 broken twill with a plain weave (55)

55 *Combined weaves,* $\frac{2}{2}$ *twill and plain weave*

(ii) *d* *Twills on a satin base* (56) A standard twill and a satin base (see chapter 3) are drafted. The twill is then put in on the satin base marks and gives high- or low-angle twills (or crêpes) according to the number of ends or picks and the satin chosen. (56) is a whipcord already given, (54*b*) considered from a different viewpoint. Diagram 57*a*–*c* shows a nine-end $\frac{4\ 1}{2\ 2}$ twill, (*a*) rearranged on a satin base, both warp way (*b*), and weft way (*c*), to give high- and low-angle twills.

56 *Seven-end whipcord constructed from a satin rearrangement of a* $\frac{3\ 1}{1\ 2}$ *twill*

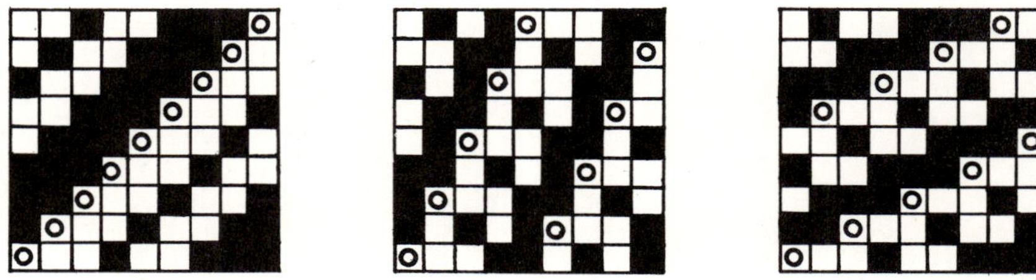

57 (*a*) *Nine-end twill* $\frac{4\ 1}{2\ 2}$
(*b*) *Rearranged on a satin base warp way*
(*c*) *Rearranged on a satin base weft way*

3 Satin weave

A satin weave gives a smooth warp-faced surface with the minimum number of stitching points, none of which are adjacent, so that there is no twill line. A sateen is a weft-faced satin, but to save confusion the two terms are now generally qualified, i.e. warp satin, and weft sateen.

A satin is produced from a twill by moving the intersections away from each other in a regular way. The twill weave moves one thread outwards on each successive pick of weft, i.e. has a move or count of 1 (*58*).

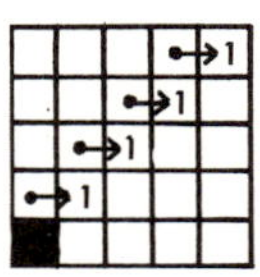

58 Five-end twill, move number of 1

A reverse twill has a move of one less than the number of ends (*59*).

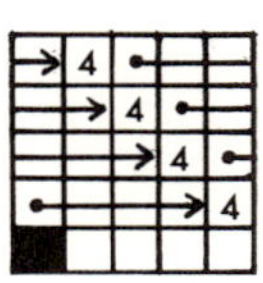

59 Five-end twill, move number of (5–1)

This leaves in the case of a five-end twill, moves of 2 and 3 (0 and 5 obviously give no weave), each of which gives a true satin (*60a, b*).

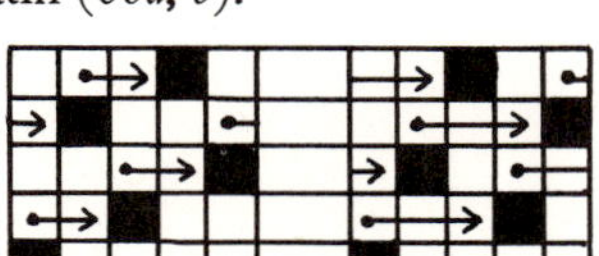

60 (a) Five-end satin, move number of 2
(b) Five-end satin, move number of 3

An eight-end satin is constructed in a similar way. Moves of 0 and 8 give no weave, moves of 2 and 6 give a weave on half the ends, a move of 4 uses only two of the ends, which leaves only moves of 3 and 5 (*61a, b*). These are left- and right-hand versions of the same weave.

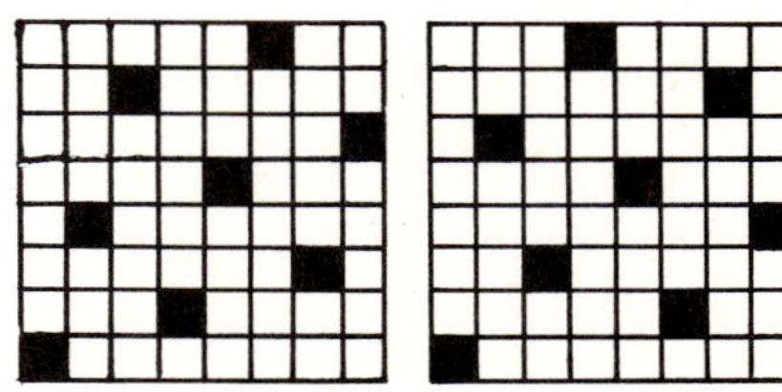

61 (a) Eight-end satin, move number of 3
(b) Eight-end satin, move number of 5

The five- and eight-end satins are probably the most useful to the handweaver. A four-end broken twill is also useful, and is the nearest to a satin that can be woven on four shafts (*62*).

62 Four-end broken twill

There is no regular satin on six ends, the nearest being almost regular, with the last two ends reversed (*63*).

63 Six-end irregular satin

It has the advantage that it is free from the slight unwanted twill which sometimes appears in a regular satin cloth. This twill needs to run in the direction of the twist in the yarn to subdue it and give a smooth unbroken cloth.

The general rule for constructing satins is that any number except for 1 and one less than the number of ends may be used for the move number, unless it will divide into the number of ends, or a smaller number will divide into both. Move numbers which together add up to the number of ends, produce right- and left-hand versions of the same weave.

4 Weaves based on plain cloth

The simplest threading for plain weave is alternately on two shafts, but a plain weave can be woven on any number of shafts, and with regular or irregular threading, provided that some combination of shafts will give all the odd ends, and another the even ends. The combination need not be even in number or regular in grouping.

This means that whenever a cloth is to be woven with a plain weave base the starting-point for planning the draft is two shafts threaded alternately. A few of the weaves derived in this way from the basic plain cloth are, extra warp and weft cloths, distorted warp, piqué, Bedford cord, traditional honeycomb, flush spot or Bronson weave, as well as all the traditional overshot and Summer and Winter weaves.

(i) A plain shaft or shafts

A good illustration of this development of a draft is the designing of a fabric with an extra weft and an extra warp, both working $\frac{3}{1}$ at intervals to form an overcheck on a plain cloth.

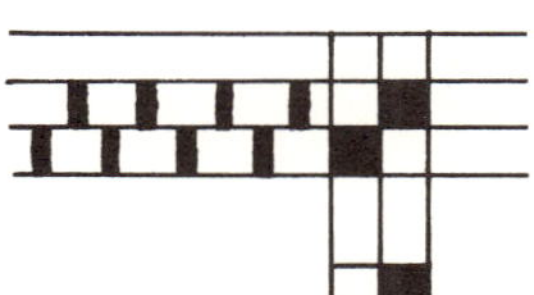

64 Plain weave on two shafts

(*65*) To provide the stitching point for the extra weft, one end in four must be controlled separately, so every fourth end is taken off shaft 1 and put on to shaft 2.

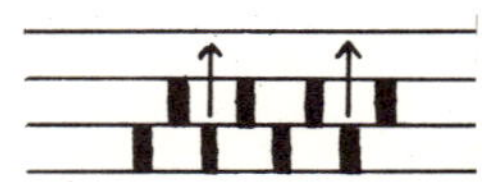

65 Plain weave with every fourth end taken off shaft 1

(*66*) This small waved draft on three shafts gives plain weave on shaft 2, then shafts 1 and 3, and the required $\frac{1}{3}$ shed for the weft to work $\frac{3}{1}$ on either shaft 1 or 3.

66 Plain weave on three shafts, point draft

(*67*) The extra warp has to be given a shaft of its own, so it can be placed on shaft 4 at intervals. To make the extra warp work $\frac{3}{1}$ this shaft must be raised for three picks and sunk for the fourth, so the weave now requires four picks to complete it, plus the extra pick at intervals for the extra weft.

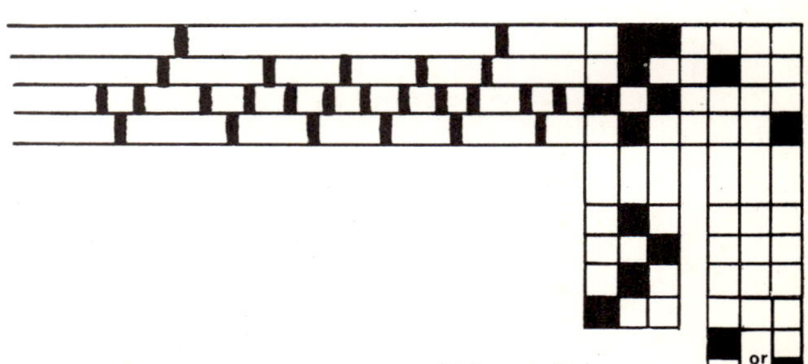

67 Extra warp added on shaft 4

(i) *a* *One plain shaft* (*68*) A general principle of drafting is to place the shafts most likely to cause trouble at the front, i.e. those most crowded with heddles, and those which work more frequently, so the original shaft 2 is brought to the front and shaft 1 moved up to 2, and the lifting plan rearranged accordingly. This gives one plain shaft and two stitching shafts.

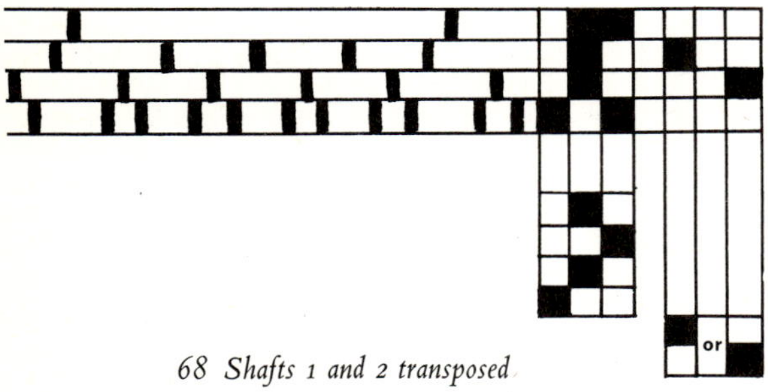

68 Shafts 1 and 2 transposed

(*69*) To widen the spaces between the stitching points another repeat of the ground weave can be placed between the stitching ends on shaft 3. The extra weft now works $\frac{5}{1}$, and the treadling plan is also modified.

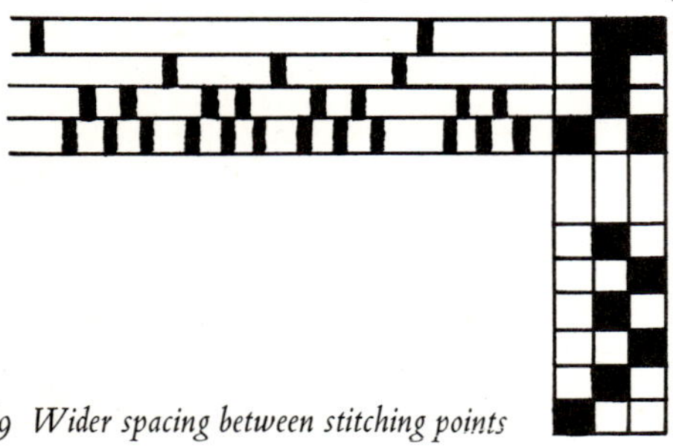

69 Wider spacing between stitching points

(*70a–d*) Shafts 2 and 3 have been transposed, but the plain weave lift is still shafts 1, then 2 and 3. In this form the weave is now recognisable as the simplest form of flush spot or Bronson weave, with the small detached spots on shaft 3, and the ends separating them on shaft 2. (*a*) shows the plain weave treadling; (*b*) the weft spot; (*c*) the warp spot; (*d*) the most practical way of planning the tie-up to use alternate feet throughout if both warp and weft spots are required in the same cloth, and to bring the heavily used plain weave treadles to the centre where less effort is required to reach them, and they are as nearly as possible an equal distance from the pivot of the lamms or marches.

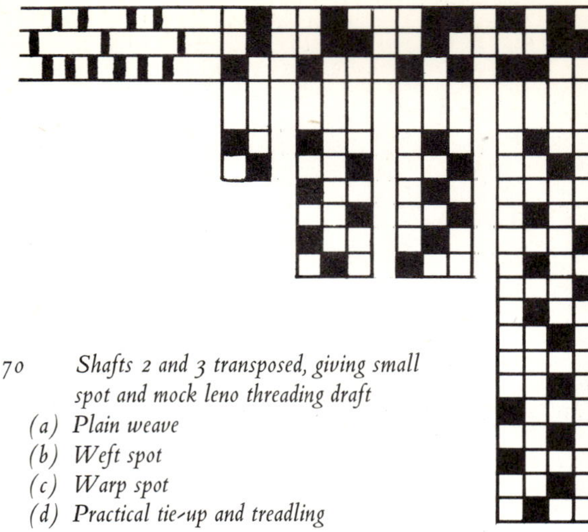

70 Shafts 2 and 3 transposed, giving small spot and mock leno threading draft
(a) Plain weave
(b) Weft spot
(c) Warp spot
(d) Practical tie-up and treadling

(*71*) By taking alternate spots from shaft 3 and placing them on shaft 4 the all-over flush spot with two half-dropped rows of spots is obtained.

71 Spot weave with two spotting shafts

(*72*) If three rows of spots are needed and a small overlap is not objectionable, shaft 2 can be given a spot instead of being used for stitching.

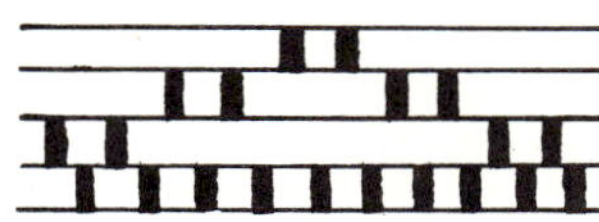

72 Spot weave with three spotting shafts

(*73*) This threading can be used to weave half-dropped rows of crosses or diamonds, or a mixture of both.

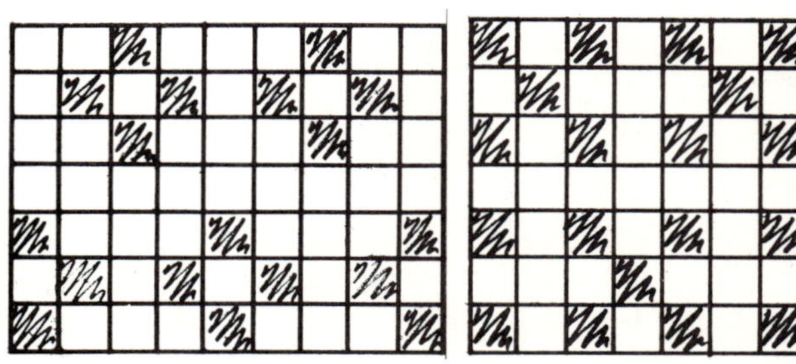

(a) Half-dropped diamonds *(b) Half-dropped crosses*

73 Block patterns for spot weave in (72)

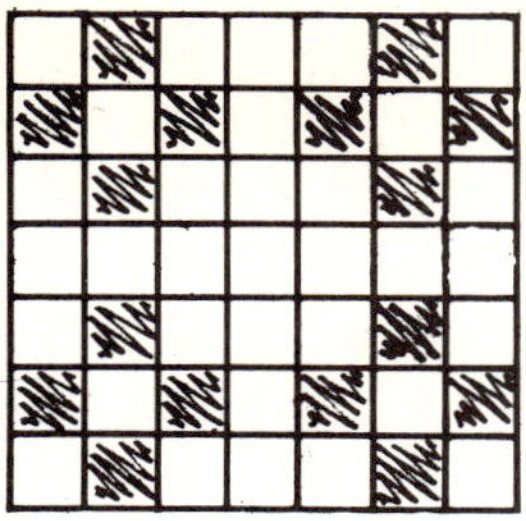

(c) Row of diamonds

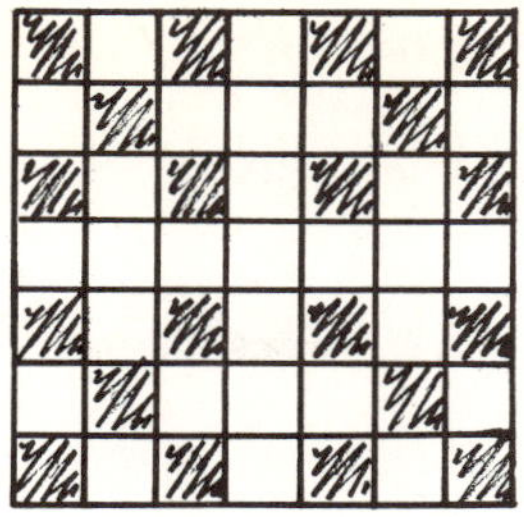

(d) Row of crosses

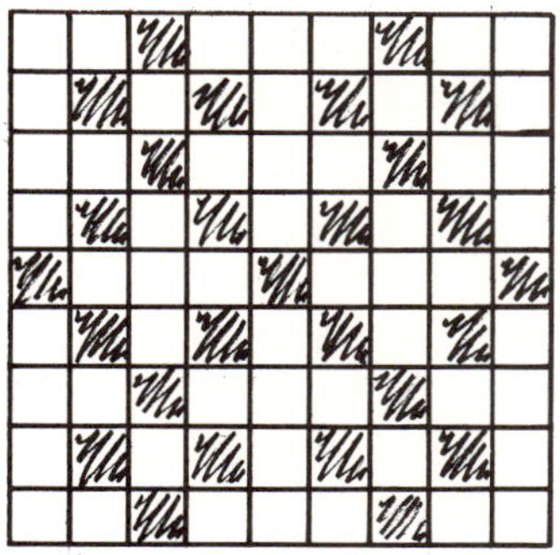

(e) Alternate rows of diamonds and crosses

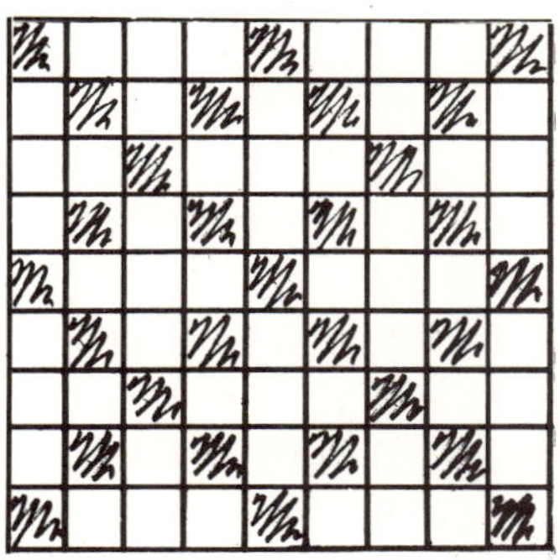

(f) Crosses with dividing spots

(74) To remove the overlap between the spots the type of threading in (71) is employed. Shaft 1 is the plain, shaft 2 the stitching shaft, and shafts 3, 4 and 5 are used for the spots. (For a counter-balanced mounting see *The Technique of Weaving*, page 23, diagram 34 paragraph f.)

74 Spot weave on five shafts; plain, stitching and three spotting shafts

(i) *b One plain shaft and one ground shaft* (75) If the spots or groups are to be completely detached, two plain shafts or, more accurately, a plain and a ground shaft are needed. The front or plain shaft carries half the ends, and the ground (second) shaft carries the background between the spots. The spots are placed on shafts 3 and 4, and can be used singly or in groups.

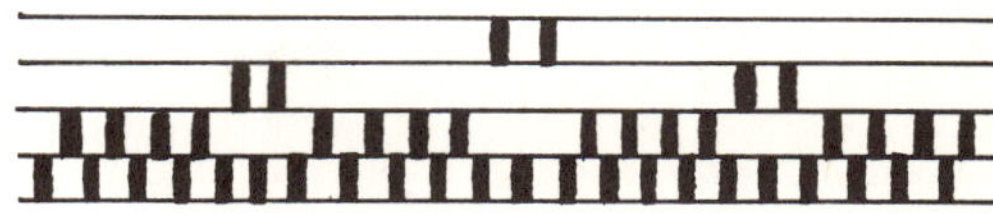

75 Spot weave with plain and ground shafts

(76) With the plain, ground, and three spotting shafts the grouping shown in (73) can be used, but can be any distance apart weft way as well as warp way. Design is now much easier as there is no need to have all the spots adjacent to each other, and the groups can be of different numbers of spots.

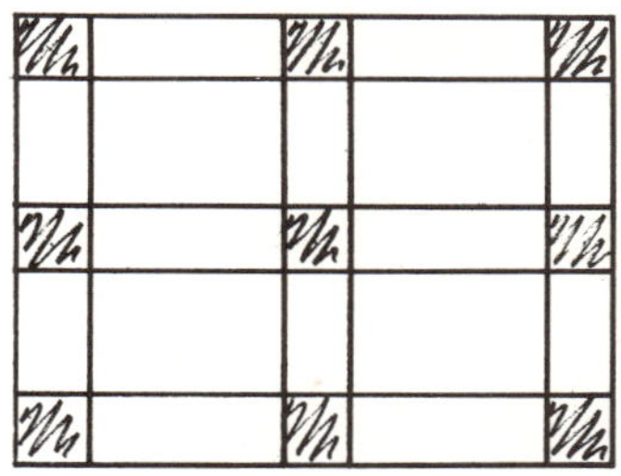

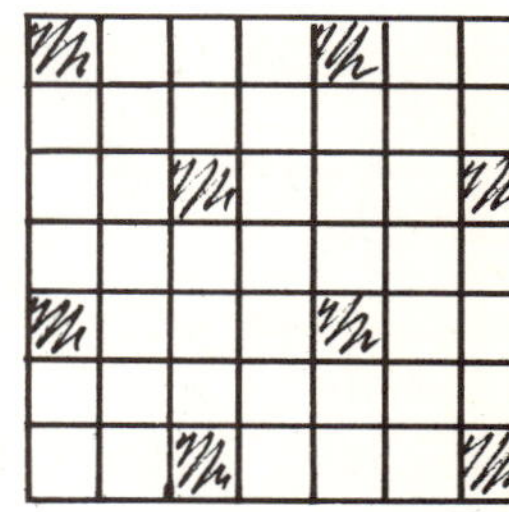

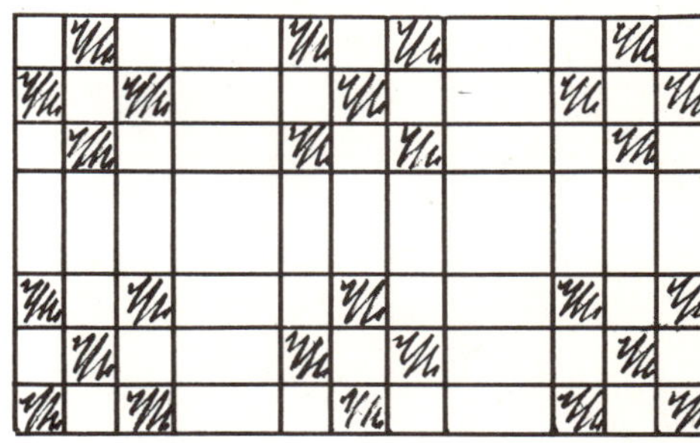

76 Block patterns for spot weaves with plain and ground shafts
(a) Single spots in rows
(b) Single spots half dropped
(c) Half-dropped rows of alternate diamonds and crosses
(d) Cloth

(*77a–d*) The lifting for all this group of weaves follows an equally straightforward plan. Plain weave is the plain shaft working against all the rest (ground and spotting). The pattern sheds for the normal weft spot are: all but one of the spotting shafts in group (i) *a*, and the same in groups (i) *b*, but with the ground shaft 2 always rising with the spotting shafts (*c*). In designs with several spotting shafts, more than one spotting shaft can be left down at times (*d*).

brought up to the face occasionally to form a spot (*b*). If the cloth being woven is more than 3 or 4 feet long (cushion-cover), the extra warp needs some means of tensioning, either with a second warp roller, which can be an improvised roller of 2 inch square wood tied securely across the back of the loom, or with warp laths packing the warp on the back roller as the slack develops (*79*).

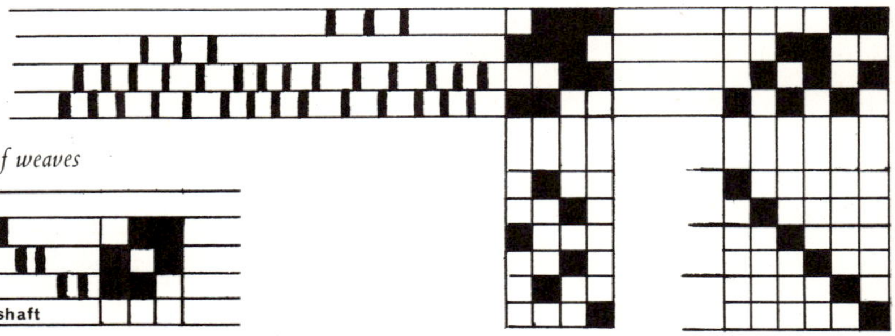

77 *Lifting plans for spot group of weaves*

(*a*) *Plain weave* (*b*) *Three spotting shafts*

78 *Extra warp*
(*a*) *Stripe*
(*b*) *Spots (half dropped)*

(*c i*) *Ground and two spotting shafts* (*c ii*) *Ground and three spotting shafts*

(*d*) *Two spotting shafts down*

The planning of spot weaves with three or more spotting shafts and a ground shaft is much more free than the usual four-shaft weave. The draft of the spots as units of design can be straight, wave, point, zigzag etc. Details of planning in blocks are given later in chapter 5 A (iii).

(ii) One pair of plain weave shafts

This section consists of plain cloths which have some form of extra warp decorating or controlling the plain cloth, and may have a weft which is not part of the cloth, but which works between the cloth and some, or all, of the extra warp. The two ground shafts carry the cloth, and the shafts behind them carry the extra warp.

(ii) *a* *Extra warp* (*78a, b*) Extra warp ends are carried on shafts behind the plain weave shafts and float either above or below the cloth, interlacing only when they change at the end of a float. They can be floated on the face with stitching points to give a solid stripe (*a*), or

79 *Extra warp combined with a distorted weft*

(ii) *b* *Distorted weft* (*80*) Plain cloth is woven for about half an inch with the warp on shaft 3 floated over the cloth. Shafts 3 and 4 are raised together and a thick weft thrown between them and the cloth. The first section is repeated, but with the warp on shaft 4 floated, and again shafts 3 and 4 are raised for the thick weft. When the cloth is washed the thick weft distorts between the warp floats (*81a, b*).

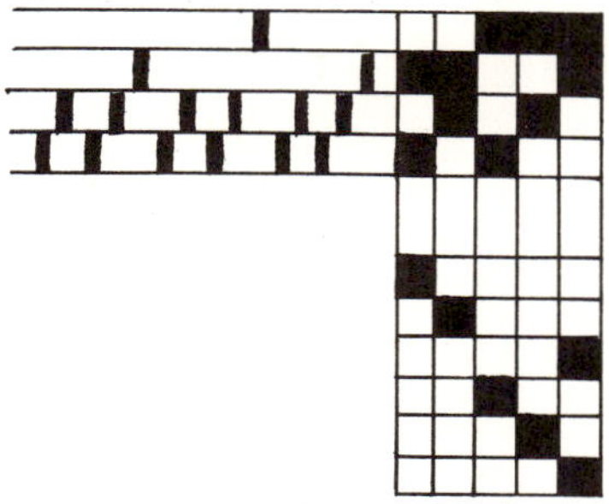

80 Distorted weft, threading and lifting drafts

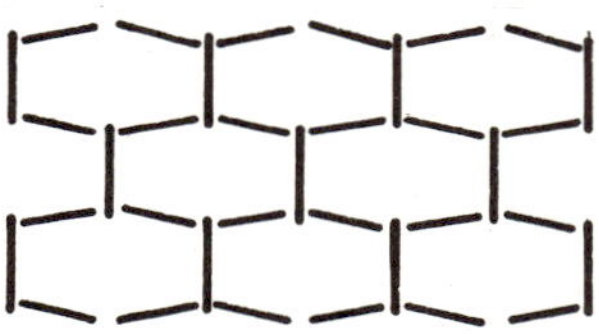

81 (a) Distorted weft, diagram
(b) Distorted weft, cloth

(*82a–c*) If the warp floats are kept fairly short, and a thick soft thread used for the extra weft, successive pattern wefts will meet under the float, to cut each section of plain weave into a series of diamonds (*a*).
Omitting every alternate row of pattern weft and using two colours for the stripes gives a waved stripe weft way (*b*). The extra warp ends are threaded 3,4,4,3,4,4, and combine with alternatives in (*a* and *b*) to give large and small diamonds (*c*).

82 Distorted weft
(a) Irregular diamonds
(b) Waved stripe
(c) Diamonds

(ii) *c* *Piqué weave* (*83*) This is a plain cloth distorted by an extra warp of stitching ends on a second warp roller which is kept strongly tensioned, the cloth being woven at a medium tension. The simple piqué or welt has horizontal ribs across the cloth separated by deep indentations. Up to three-quarters of an inch of plain is woven with the stitching ends down, and then two picks with them up. As the stitching ends are tight the cloth slides along them, and a cord rib is thrown up. The rib can be accentuated by inserting a wadding pick between the cloth and the stitching ends half-way through the weaving of each rib. This gives a 'loose back' piqué. If the floats of the stitching ends are long enough to catch in use, the alternative threading (*84*) enables a pair of wadding picks to be woven plain through the stitching ends on the back of the fabric to give a 'fast back' piqué.

83 Piqué weave diagram

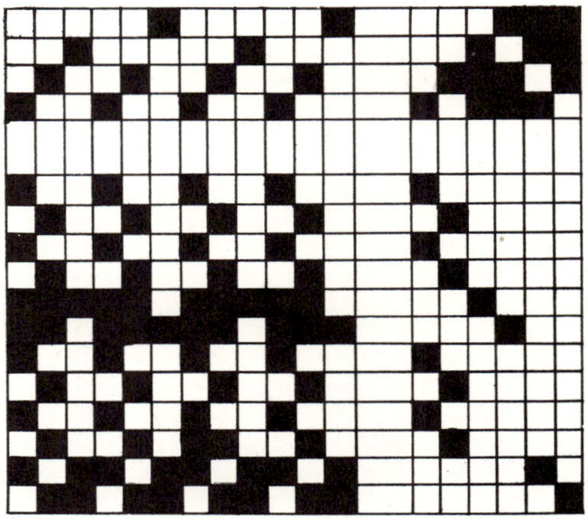

84 Piqué weave diagram, alternative threading for fast back

(*85a, b*) A waved piqué is similar, except that the stitching ends form a diamond pattern (*a*), and the wadding picks go between the diamonds. The diamonds do not overlap horizontally, one row ending as the next begins. It is rather like the distorted weft in section (ii) *b* above, with the extra weft on the back, and a more complicated arrangement of extra warp ends (*b*) and (*86*).
In all piqué weaves the warp ends should be sleyed with the stitching end between two ground ends in each dent of the reed.

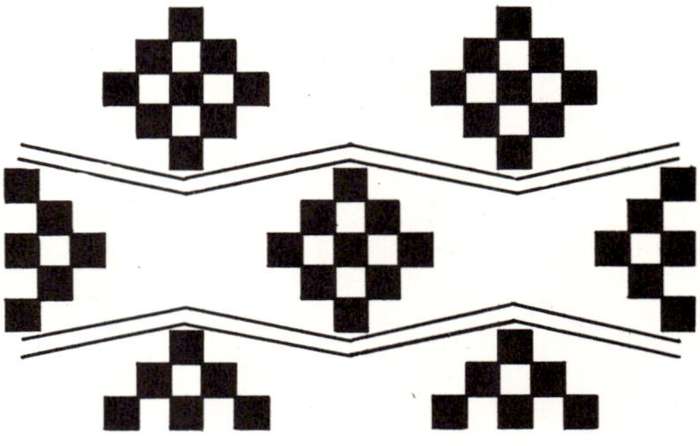

(b) Diagram

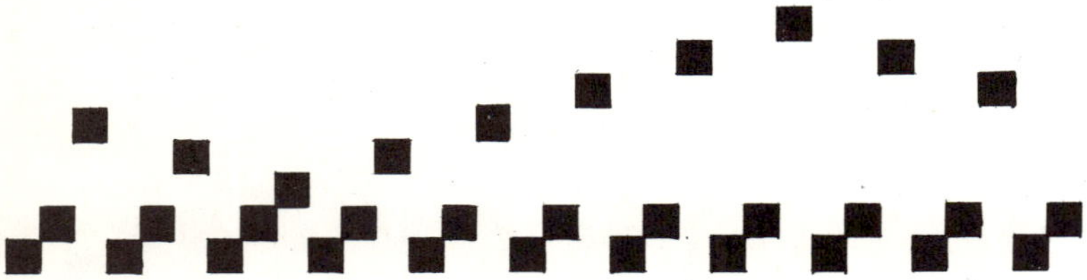

85 Waved piqué
(a) Threading draft

86 *Waved piqué, heavy woollen coat fabric*

(iii) Two pairs of plain weave shafts

(*87a–h*) By threading short sections of warp on the front pair or back pair of shafts alternately, as well as being used to give plain weave right across the cloth (*a*), two sections can be controlled independently of each other; (*b*) Shows the simple reversal of the weave, the odd ends of one set rising with the even ends of the other; (*c*) shows one set being woven while the other is left down to be covered by a floating weft; (*d*) is a similar weave but with the second set raised to float over the weft; (*e*) one set held open for a complete check while the other set is woven; (*f*) one set weaving plain while the other sheds after every third pick; (*g*) both sets shedding three picks plain, three picks as one; (*h*) sections raised in blocks without any plain weave; (*i*) samples woven with some of the above weaves. All the following weaves are based on some combination of these.

87 *Two pairs of plain weave shafts, alternative lifting plans*

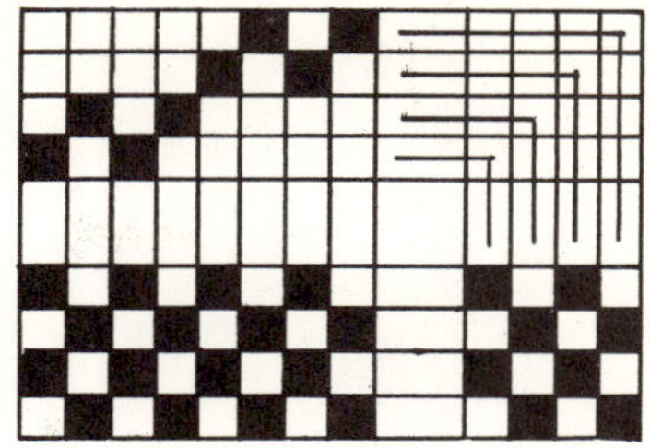

(a) Plain weave on both sets

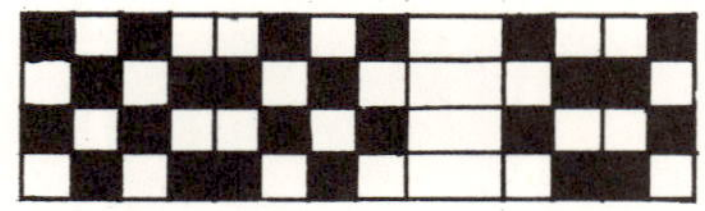

(b) Plain weave on both sets, second set reversed lifting

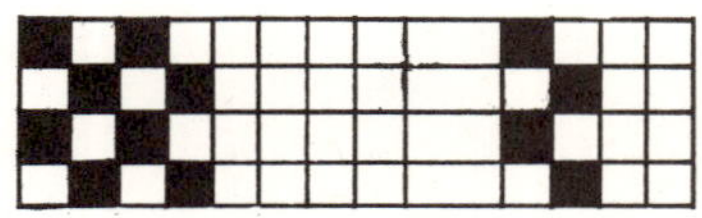

(c) Plain weave on one set, other set left down

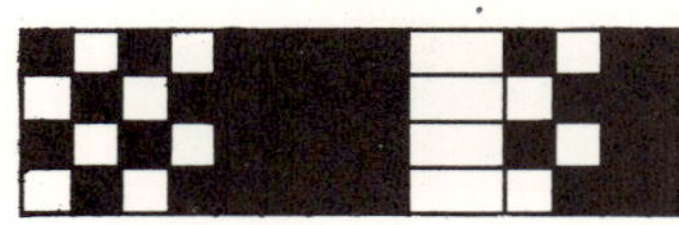

(d) Plain weave on one set, other set left up

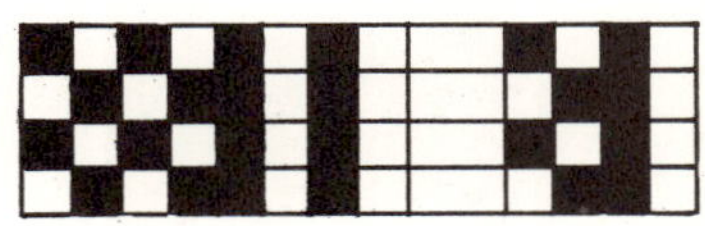

(e) Plain weave on one set, other set held open

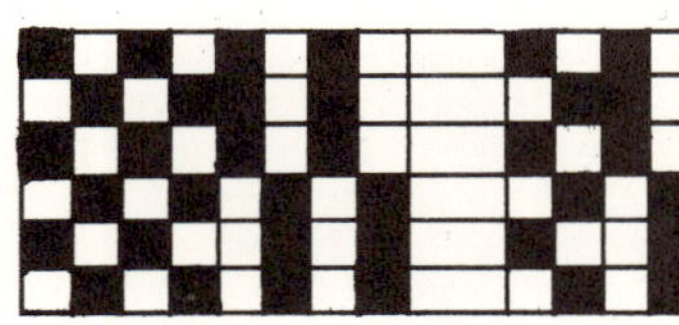

(f) Plain weave on one set, other shedding after every third pick

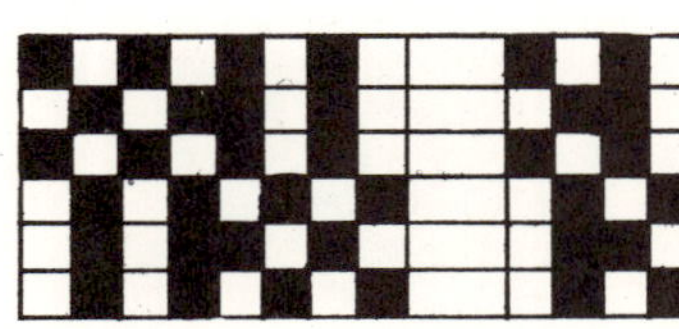

(g) Both sets shedding three picks plain, three picks as one

(h) Sections raised in blocks without any plain weave

87 (i) Samples woven with some of the above weaves

(iii) *a* *Extra weft, lifting* (*h*), (*c*), (*d*) When either the odd or even blocks of warp are raised, an extra weft floats below or above each block, giving a series of horizontal lines which are not tied into the fabric (*h*). The extra weft can be woven through one set and floated above or below the other set which ties the weft in but causes it to show on the face of the cloth (*c*) or (*d*). The extra weft is most useful combined with other weaves, e.g. with extra warp (see section (ii) *a*) to give a coarse plain weave on a finer ground (see section (iii)).

(iii) *b* *Distorted warp*, (*h*), (*c*) Thick extra ends on a separate beam (see section (ii) *a*) float over all the cloth, but under extra picks which are woven either above and below the sets of warp (*h*), or floated over one set and woven through the other (*c*). The extra ends are drawn between the sets of warp, and distort weft way in the finishing as the extra weft distorted warp way. Diagram *88* is the threading draft, *89* the extra ends and picks, *90* a cloth woven using only the odd numbered extra ends.

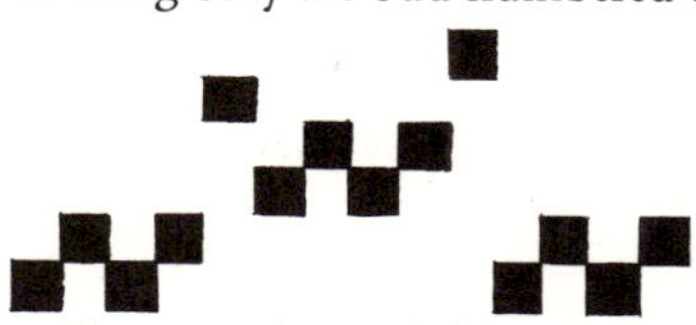

88 Distorted warp threading draft

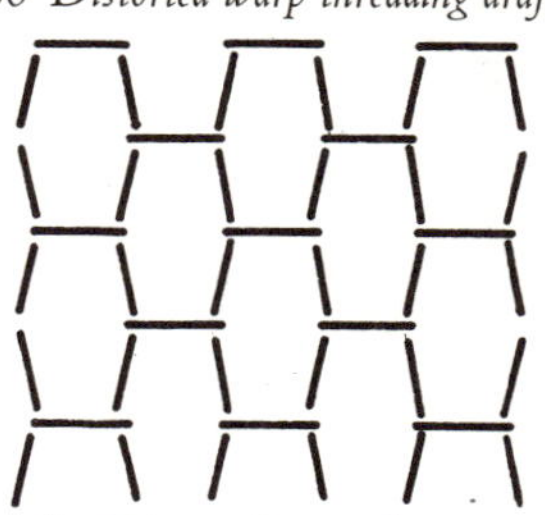

89 Distorted warp diagram

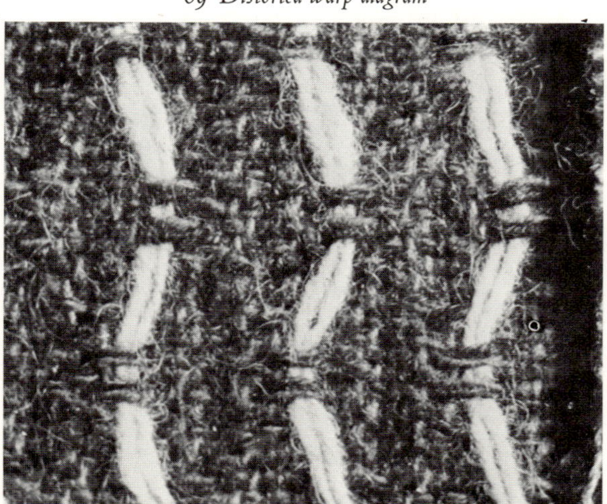

90 Distorted warp

(iii) *c* *Bedford cord* (*d*) This is similar in effect to a piqué but with the cords running warp way instead of the ribs weft way, though the principle underlying it is completely different. Instead of using an extra set of threads to distort the cloth, the weft itself distorts alternate sets. A true Bedford cord requires six shafts (q.v.), but a good cloth can be woven on four. The odd picks weave through the odd sections and the even picks through the even sections, and in each case float below the section in which they are not working (*d*). In finishing the plain weave expands, tightening the floating weft on the back, and so throwing the fabric into cords.

91 Bedford cord cross-section

(*91*) A true Bedford cord has the cords separated by pairs of plain weave ends to give a cutting line. These ends are drawn on the front pair of shafts, and the weave of the cord ends matches the weave on the plain ends. It is also woven with wadding ends to help to raise the cord. These ends are thicker than the warp, and are on a second warp beam (see section (ii) *a*). They run between the face of the cloth and the weft floats on the back, and are dented in addition to the cord ends. As they never rise above the cord ends this causes no trouble. The cloth is usually woven two picks of each stripe instead of alternate picks. Shafts 7 and 8 give the threading and lifting for the wadding ends, and can be omitted without altering the rest of the draft (*92*).

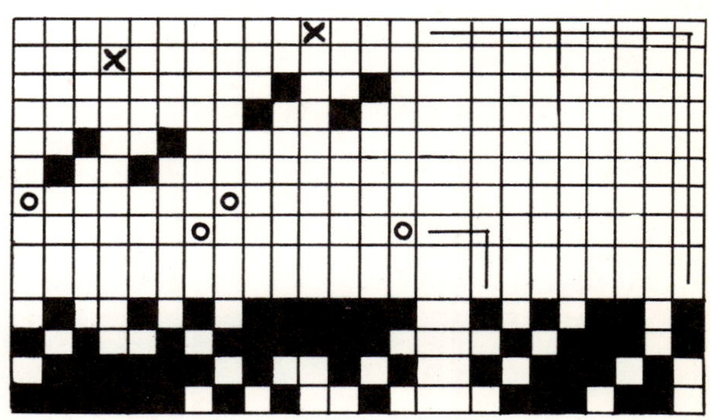

92 Bedford cord weave diagram

(iii) *d* *Repp check* (*93*) If the warp is drawn in odd ends thick, even ends thin, right across, a plain weave using a thick and thin weft (*a*) will give an unbroken repp weave. If the blocks on the back pair of shafts are lifted in the opposite way to the front pair (*b*), the repp will be

93 Repp check

broken where the blocks join, and the face of the repp will be thrown to the back of the cloth on alternate stripes. By throwing two fine (or coarse) picks in successive sheds the weave can be broken weft way, and a check pattern of texture, or colour and texture can be developed. The check can, of course, be woven on two shafts by breaking the order of threading at the edges of the check, but by placing alternate stripes on a second pair of shafts isolated squares on a plain ground can be woven.

(iii) *e* *Traditional honeycomb*, (*d*) and (*a*) (*94*) A short length of about half an inch is woven on one section of warp, and the other set held up. Two picks of thick weft are thrown right across the cloth in plain weave, and the weave repeated on the second section, finishing with another pair of thick plain weave picks (*d* and *a*). It is better woven face down as then fewer threads are raised and there is less strain on both warp and mounting. Variations can be woven on 6 and 8 shafts.

94 Traditional honeycomb

(iii) *f* *Imitation leno*, (*e*), (*f*), (*g*) A leno weave is based on some form of crossing weave, but instead of the crossing ends crossing on each pick, they work in some form of weave on the open or the crossed side of the standard end (see chapter 9). There are several weaves which imitate gauze or leno, and this particular group imitates what is known as two-doup fabric, which needs two complete sets of gauze mounting combined into one.

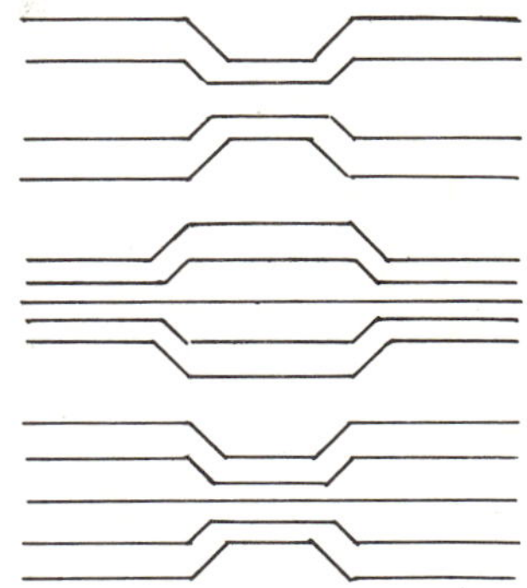

95 Imitation leno weave, (e) diagram 87

95 is weave (e), which can be used only on a small scale, otherwise there is too much disparity between the outer and middle picks working together.

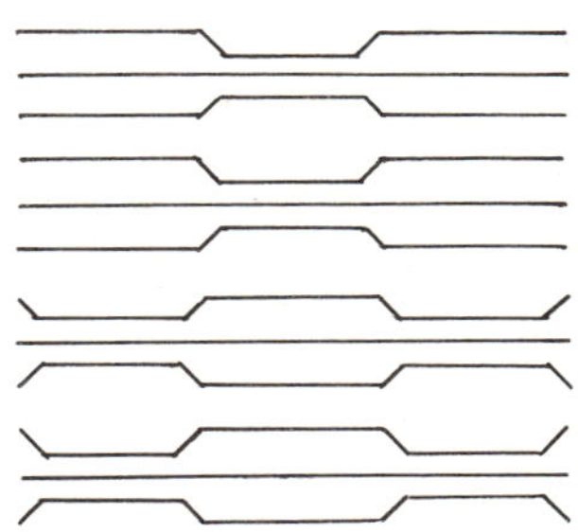

96 Imitation leno weave, (f) diagram 87

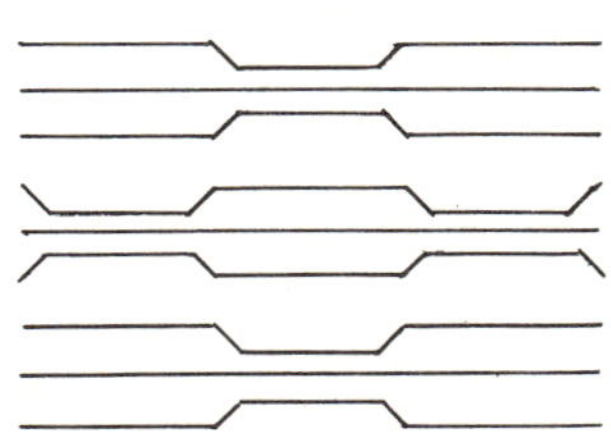

97 Imitation leno weave, (g) diagram 87

96 is weave (*f*) 97 is weave (*g*). Both can be used for all-over texturing, and there is no tension trouble in either unless the blocks in (*f*) are made too long.

(iii) *g* *Modified rib and cord weaves* Plain rib and cord weaves were discussed in chapter 1, section (i). *b* and *c* as extensions of plain weave warp way or weft way. They can be woven on two pairs of plain weave shafts to produce small all-over textures. In any one weave both sections have the same lifting plan, but one section is half dropped relative to the other.

98 (*a*) shows $\frac{2}{2}$ warp rib; (*b*) $\frac{4}{4}$ warp rib; (*c*) $\frac{3}{1}$ warp rib on six ends; (*d*) $\frac{3}{1}$ warp rib on five ends to give more warp face. A $\frac{5}{1}$ rib as (*c*) is known as a Barathea when woven in fine smooth yarns, e.g. for a silk necktie fabric. (*N.B.* in this case the $\frac{2}{2}$, etc. is the way the *warp* threads work upwards.)

98 Warp ribs

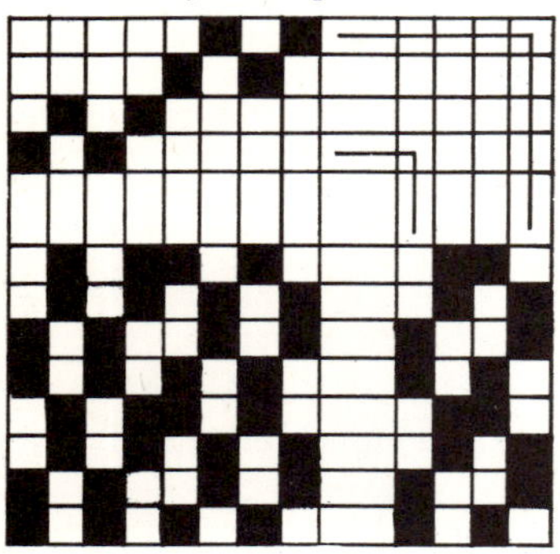

(*a*) $\frac{2}{2}$

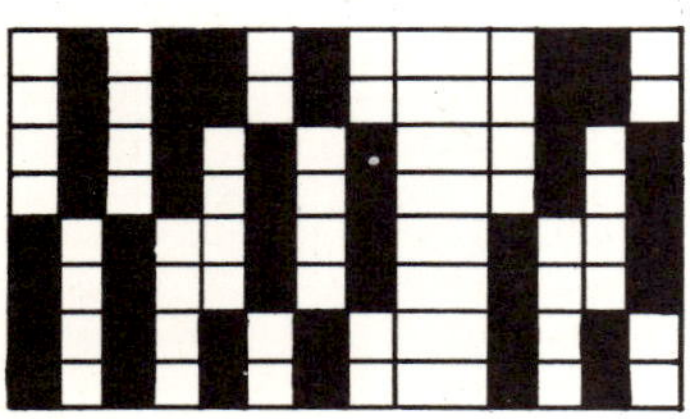

(*b*) $\frac{4}{4}$

(*c*) *Six-end*, $\frac{3}{1}$

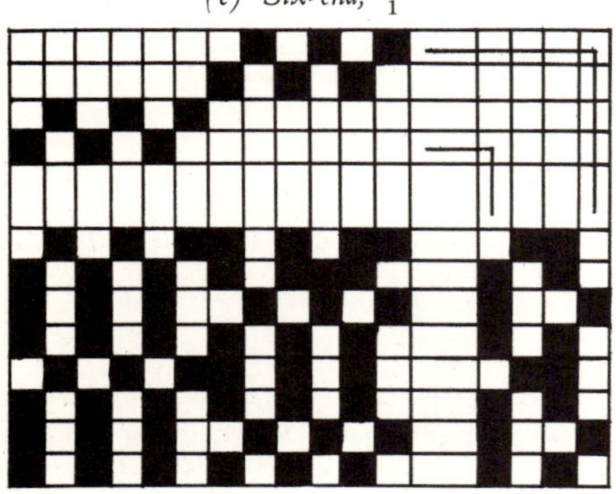

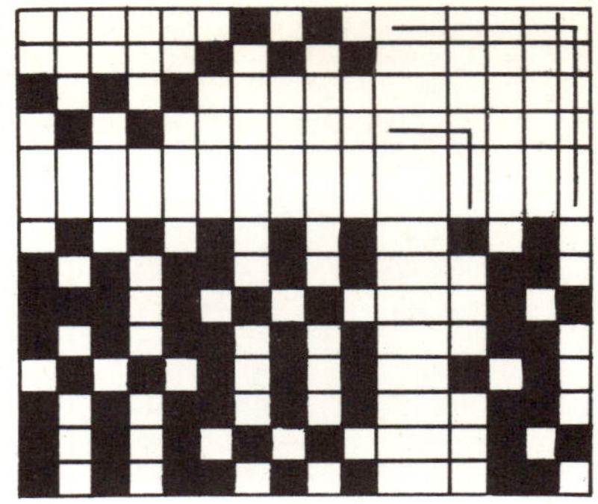

(*d*) *Five-end*, $\frac{3}{1}$

Cords or weft ribs are the same weave turned round from warp way to weft way and need a different threading from the warp ribs. A $\frac{3}{1}$ cord corresponding to (*c*) above is shown in (*99a*), and a modification of it which gives a slight piqué effect in (*99b*).

99 Weft cords

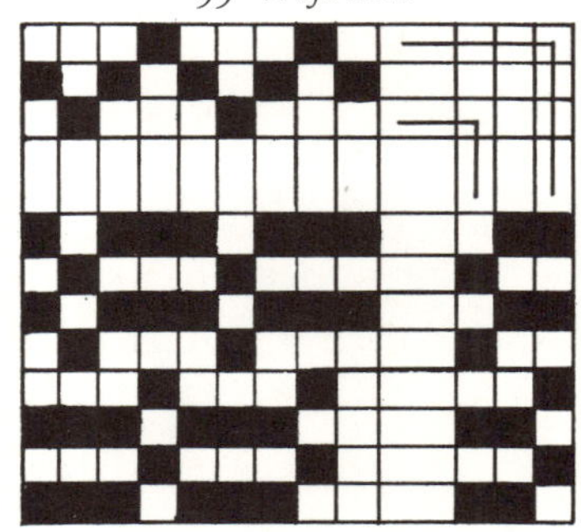

(*a*) $\frac{3}{1}$

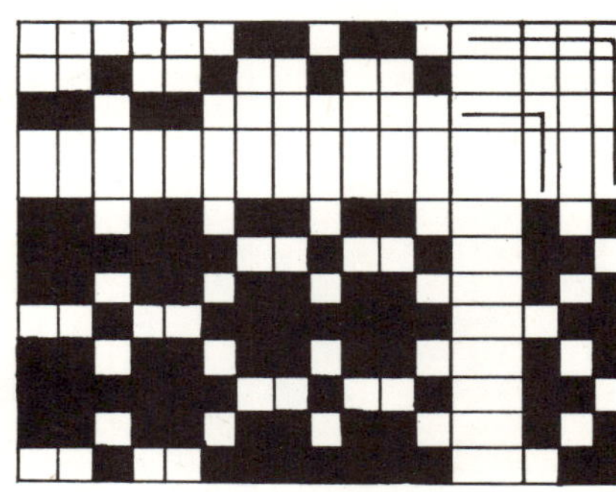

(*b*) *Modified* $\frac{3}{1}$

(iv) Three pairs of plain weave shafts

This covers the same range of weaves, but with three different alternatives. Any two blocks can be woven as one, which extends the design possibilities (see chapter 5 A section (iii) (*100*) and (*101*).

100 Three block honeycomb

101 Three block extra weft spot

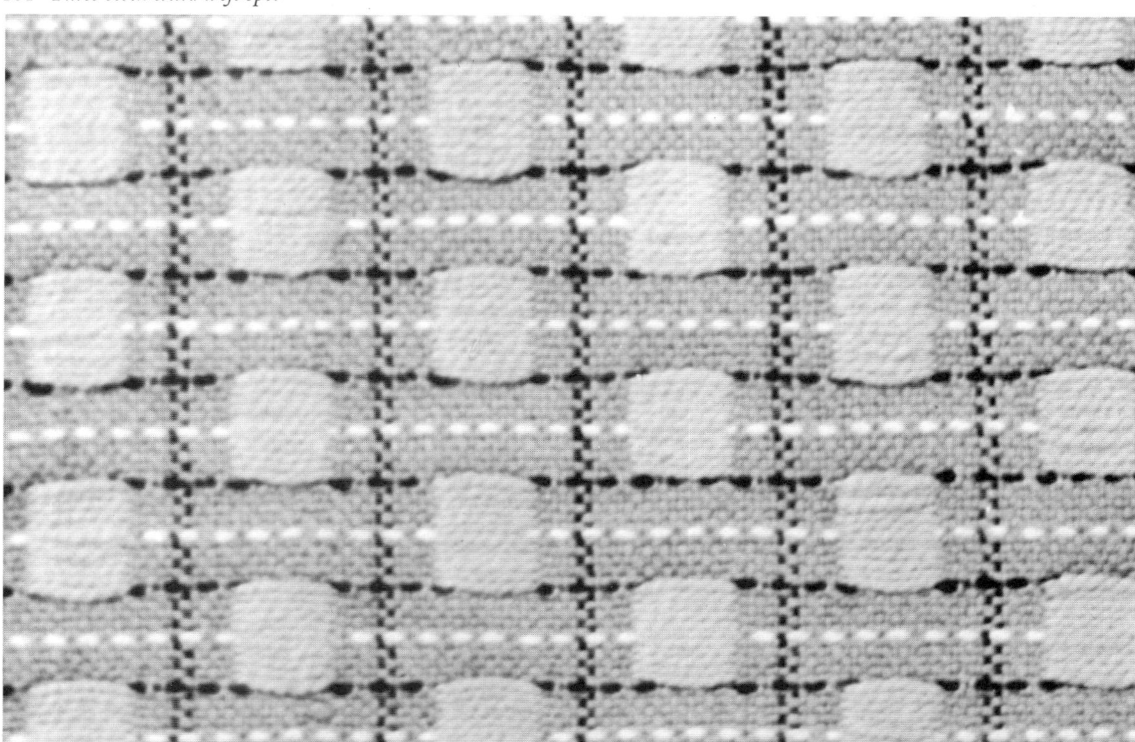

(v) Combined weaves

Coarse weave in extra warp and weft on plain fabric.

Often two or more of the previous weaves can be combined in the same cloth. By combining an extra warp section (ii) *a* with an extra weft section (iii) *a*, both in thick yarns, a coarse weave on a fine ground is woven.

(*102a–c*) (*a*) extra warp; (*b*) extra weft; (*c*) both combined.

102 Combined weaves, extra warp and extra weft

(*a*) *Extra warp*
(*b*) *Extra weft*
(*c*) *Both combined*

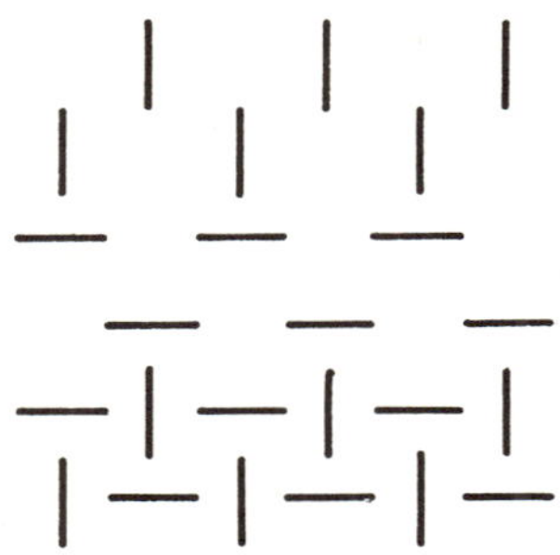

(*103*) coarse weave with doubled ends and picks.

103 Coarse weave with doubled ends and picks on plain ground

A traditional honeycomb and can have threads floating over the hollow by adding weave (*c*). The sections need to have an odd number of threads for the best effect.

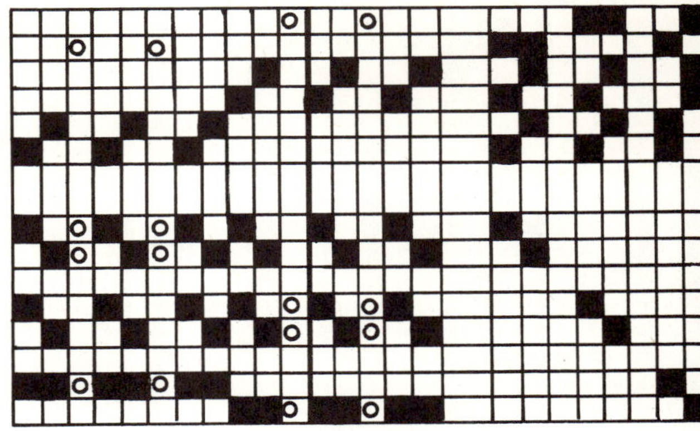

104 Threading draft for (103)

5 Overshot and allied weaves

A Overshot weaves

The traditional overshot weave consists of a plain weave ground with a pattern weft floating above or below it, but never strictly part of the cloth in the sense that the picks of weft in a twill weave are part of the cloth. The pattern could be cut away completely and a perfectly sound cloth would remain. It is in the same class as the broché weave, a cheap form of brocade used in the seventeenth and eighteenth centuries.

Overshot patterns fall into a few well-defined groups, and once the basic construction of each group is understood, designing new patterns or modifying old ones becomes straightforward.

The two main subdivisions of four-shaft overshot patterns are, four blocks on adjacent pairs of shafts, and two blocks on opposites. The latter can be used in two different ways, either as an all-over pattern, or to produce modified forms of the four-block patterns.

There are other weaves somewhat similar in effect but different in construction, e.g. Summer and Winter, Crackle weave, Bronson, Ms and Os, etc., and these are discussed under the appropriate headings. Eight-shaft overshot weaves are usually an extension of four-shaft, alternate sections of warp being threaded on the front four or back four shafts, so that they can be controlled separately though woven simultaneously.

(i) Two blocks on opposite pairs of shafts

(*105*) The simplest technically is the plain two-block on opposites. The starting point is the plain weave threading on two shafts, which gives only plain weave right across the warp.

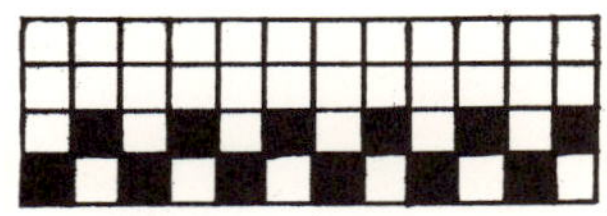

105 *Plain weave on two shafts*

(*106*) If a group of threads is taken off shafts 1 and 2 and put on to shafts 3 and 4, this group can be raised or sunk as a unit by working together the front and back pairs of shafts, plain weave being unaffected as it is obtained from the odd and even pairs of shafts.

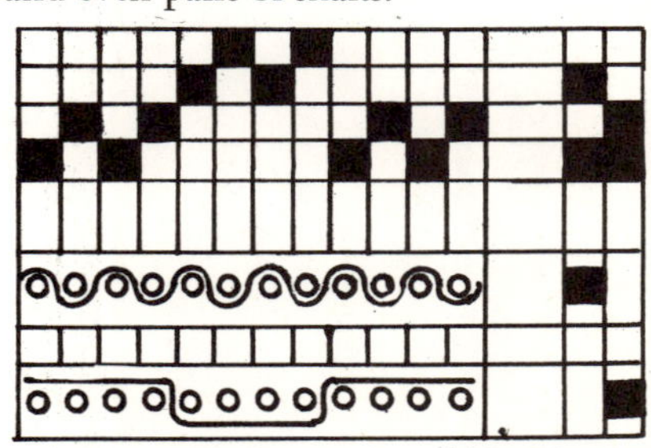

106 *Two-block threading with cross-sections of sheds*

(*107*) The pattern weft floats over the ground but is never tied in. This gives clear-cut blocks of pattern and ground colour alternately.

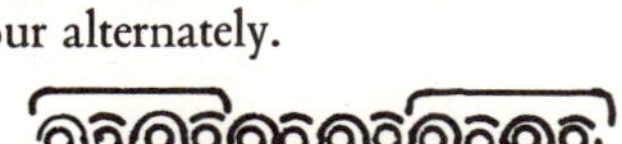

107 *Two-block cloth, cross-section*

(i) *a Simple two-block patterns* This group of designs consists entirely of checks of two colours, pattern and ground, like a chess-board with squares and rectangles of differing proportions, and covers the whole width of the cloth. The smallest unit of design is two warp ends, and the largest depends on the sett of the cloth, about three-quarters of an inch with a fairly heavy sett and weft. The proportions can vary considerably within a pattern though, generally speaking, two sizes of unit for small designs and three for large designs are sufficient, except for special effects.

108 (*a*) two sizes of unit repeated (*i*) one large one small; (*ii*) one large two small; (*iii*) one large three small
(*b*) two sizes of unit (*i*) three large two small; (*ii*) three large three small
(*c*) the two main sizes of unit are both subdivided, partly for design, and partly structurally to prevent excessive length of float.
This type is most often used for borders on table-linen, household furnishings, and graduated borders on skirts. A well-known pattern of this type is Monk's Belt.

108 Two-block designs
(a) Small and large single units (i), (ii), (iii)

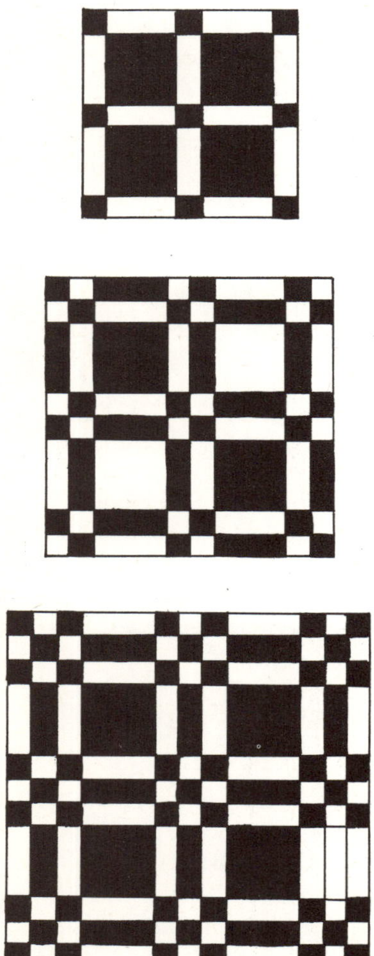

(b) Small units with large subdivided units (i), (ii)

(c) Small and large units, both subdivided

(i) *b* *Modified four-block* (*109*) When taking alternate sections of warp out of plain weave shafts to give two-block threading, the obvious choice is the front and back pairs of shafts, but the inside and outside pairs could equally well be chosen. Both pattern pairs can be combined in the same draft in two ways.

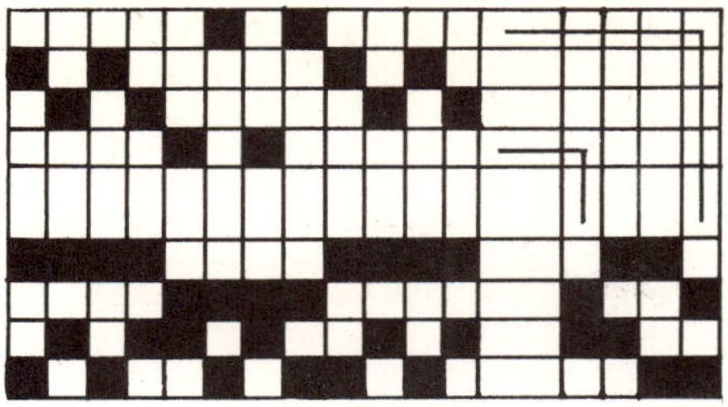

109 Two-block threading on inside and outside pairs

111 Turning four-block pattern on opposites
(a i) Threading
(a ii) Block design
(b) Block pattern

1 *Table figures* (*110*) In designs based on two large subdivided units, one set of opposite pairs of shafts is given to each unit, e.g. front and back, shafts 1 and 2, 3 and 4 for the smaller; inside and outside, shafts 2 and 3, 4 and 1 for the larger. While one unit is woven the pattern weft works plain through the width of the next unit, except for the two-end floats which occur where the blocks join, (*111 a*) draft, (*b*) pattern.

110 Four-block design on two sets of opposite shafts

2 Running figures (*112*) In designs based on a series of diagonal lines of squares or rectangles the blocks run on front, back, inside and outside pairs, (shafts 1 and 2, 3 and 4, 2 and 3, 4 and 1), and give the effect of a pattern line flanked by a ground line on a half-tone background.

The general effect of patterns on opposites is brilliant compared with the more subdued standard four blocks, but they are often inclined to look broken if too many small blocks are used, as the double floats on the half-tone background are too prominent. Patterns of the modified four-block group are used as the standard four-block patterns, usually for furnishing fabrics, cushion-covers, etc.

112 Running four-block pattern on opposites

(ii) Four blocks on adjacent pairs of shafts

The four-block patterns on four shafts need all four pairs of shafts remaining after the two pairs for plain weave have been allowed for. The most common way of drafting uses the odds and evens (shafts 1 and 3, 2 and 4) for plain weave, and the pairs shafts 1 and 2, 2 and 3, 3 and 4, 4 and 1 for the pattern. This is based on the straight draft. Some handweavers prefer to use the satin draft as the basis of planning the blocks, and in this case the plain weave will be shafts 1 and 2, 3 and 4, and the pattern blocks shafts 2 and 3, 1 and 3, 1 and 4, 4 and 2. At least one well-known book uses this system, and to alter it to the straight draft basis shafts 2 and 3 have to be transposed. Although the satin draft has advantages mechanically, it is easier to 'read' the shape of a pattern from a straight draft.

(*113*) The easiest way to think of the sequence of blocks in a draft is to write the shaft numbers down in a circle with the 1 at the top. Each block is now formed from the shaft of the same number and the next one higher (clockwise). To differentiate shafts from blocks the shafts will be Arabic numerals and the blocks Roman.

Plain weave pairs will be referred to as (A) odd (1 and 3), and (B) even (2 and 4).

Shafts	Block
1 and 2	I
2 and 3	II
3 and 4	III
4 and 1	IV
1 and 3	A
2 and 4	B

As the pattern weft is the most prominent set of threads in the overshot weaves, for the remainder of this chapter the tie-up and treadling will indicate sinking plans, and the weave plan will be weft marks to rise. Thus the cloth will be woven face upwards on the loom, and the development of the pattern can be followed as it is woven.

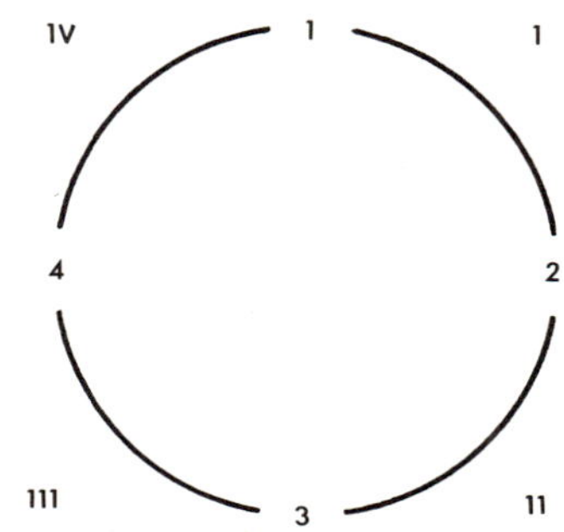

113 Numbering of shafts and blocks

114 is a simple threading to illustrate the essentials of the four-block pattern. Block I has four ends on shafts 1,2,1,2. Block II uses the last end of block I and adds three more to give 2,3,2,3. Block III, using the end common with block II is 3,4,3,4, and block IV is 4,1,4,1. The last block is I again. Each block is joined to the next by the common end, which is of course on the shaft common to the two blocks, i.e. shaft 2 joins I and II, and shaft 4 joins III and IV.

(*115*) When 1 and 2 are sunk together the first four ends go down as a unit. The next end on 3 rises, and the next on 2 again sinks. The four ends on 3 and 4 rise as a unit, and the following ends on 1 and 4 sink and rise respectively. Finally, the four ends on 1 and 2 sink again. The pattern pick therefore floats above I (1 and 2), works plain through II (2 and 3), floats below III (3 and 4) and works plain through IV (4 and 1). Thus I is pattern, III is ground, and II and IV are half-tone. The blocks are numbered on the draft, and the sections above and below the weave plan are picks 1 and 2 from the weave plan. At no time does the pattern weft go from face to back of the cloth as it does in two block patterns on opposites, so there is never any sharply defined edge. Each block of solid colour, either pattern or ground, has a block of half-tone on all four sides which blend in with the next colour.

114 Four-block overshot threading

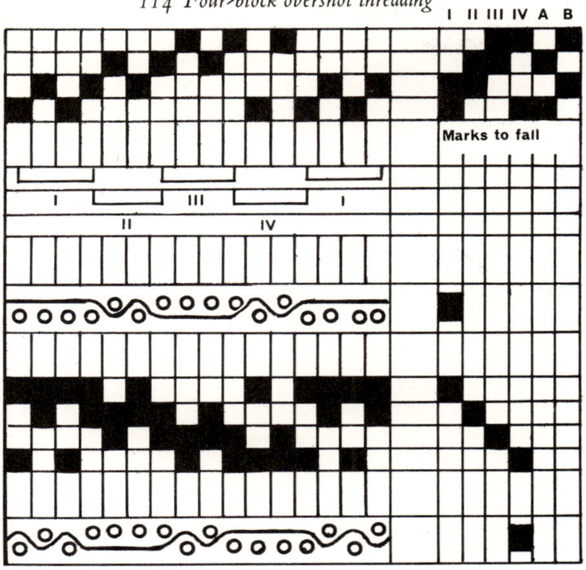

115 Block weave plan of (114); cross-sections of blocks I and IV

The blocks are of two types, running and turning. (*116*) Running blocks are part of a line, and have an even number of ends because they are entered and left by different shafts at diagonally opposite corners.

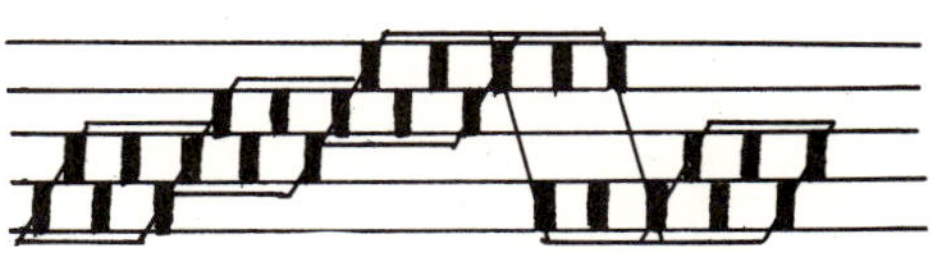

116 Running blocks draft

(*117a, b*) Turning blocks are entered and left by the same shaft at both front or back corners, and therefore have an odd number of ends. As well as being the blocks about which units are symmetrical, turning blocks can be used in two other ways. They can form solid blocks or 'tables' of fairly small even checks, such as where the border and cross-border of a large pattern meet, or between smaller and more open units of a repeating design, and they can be sub-units of a larger pattern.

In each case the unit is drafted on three shafts, the centre one common to both sets of blocks, and the other two taking the rest of the ends between them, alternately behind and in front of the common shaft.

All the traditional overshot patterns are built up from some combination of running and turning blocks, which form comparatively few easily recognisable design units.

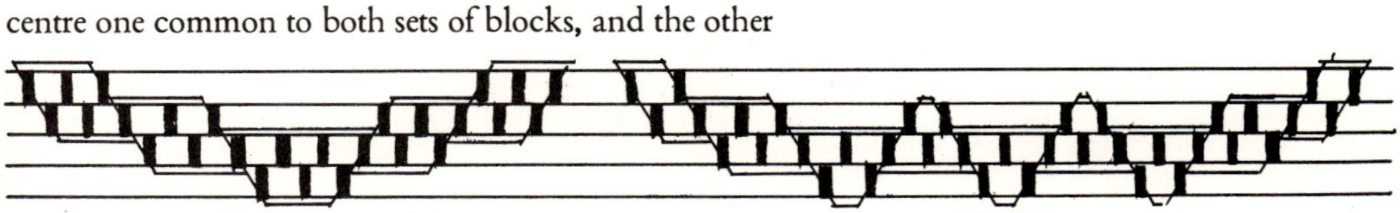

117 Turning blocks draft (a) Turning-point (b) Table

118 Snail's Trail

(ii) *a Running blocks* Running blocks, like twills, can be drafted to give straight, point or waved designs.

The straight draft occurs most frequently as part of a larger pattern such as Snail's Trail (*118*) or Finnish Figure, though there are good patterns based on a straight draft.

A point draft, strictly speaking, reverses only once at the centre of the cloth, and this, with a reversal of lifting half-way through the weaving gives either a series of concentric diamonds (*119*), or a design based on a diagonal cross with diminishing chevrons between the arms of the cross (*120*). These are quite useful weaves for small household articles.

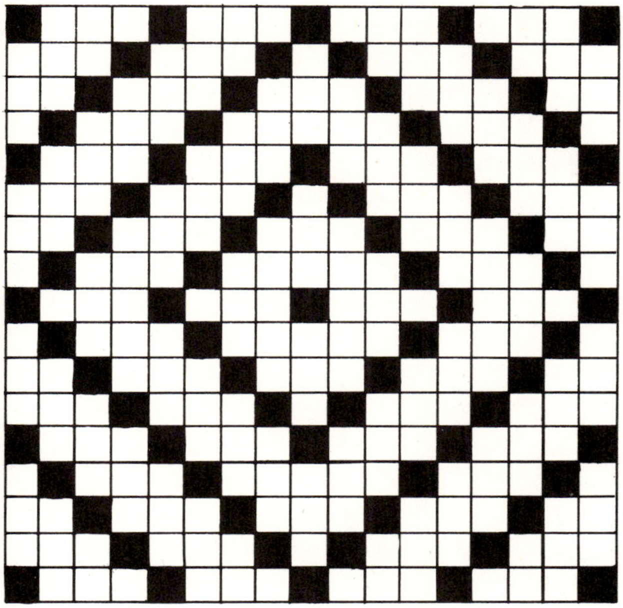

119 Running blocks, diamond lifting

120 Running blocks, cross lifting

The waved draft gives, as well as the obvious series of equal or zigzag waves, an all-over pattern of diamonds. If each repeat is divided by a table (see Section (ii) *b* (*1* below) it becomes, in effect, a small point, and can be woven as a cross or diamond. The cross formation gives rise to a series of patterns such as the Sunrise figures, and the Blooming Leaf or Bow Knot figures; the diamond gives the wheels such as Chariot Wheel and, in a modified version, Wheel of Fortune.

There are four possibilities for designs with running blocks.

1 Equal blocks (*121*) These give the straightforward diamond patterns. The turning blocks are usually one end more than the running blocks, rather than less, to give a more satisfactory visual balance. It is better to weave the patterns square, which usually means one thread less warp way than weft way because of the overlap, but if for any reason the cloth is designed with warp and ground weft of different counts the pattern should be woven to look correct, with the diagonal lines of pattern at 45 degrees, or slightly higher (to lengthen the pattern) if the exact angle proves impracticable, as this is more satisfactory than the cramped effect of a lower angle.

121 Running blocks equal, diamond pattern

2 Blocks decreasing to the centre of the unit (*122a, b*) Commencing with a large block and decreasing in size towards the centre strengthens the corners and gives a bold pattern with a strong diagonal cross filled in with curved chevrons between the arms of the cross. If the extreme blocks at the corners have too long a float stitching points can be inserted (see tables) without destroying the pattern. It can be used on a large scale with a table (q.v.) replacing the corner block in a cushion-cover or, on a small scale, as a repeating pattern with dividing tables.

122 Running blocks decreasing to centre, cross lifting
(*a*) *Curved line*

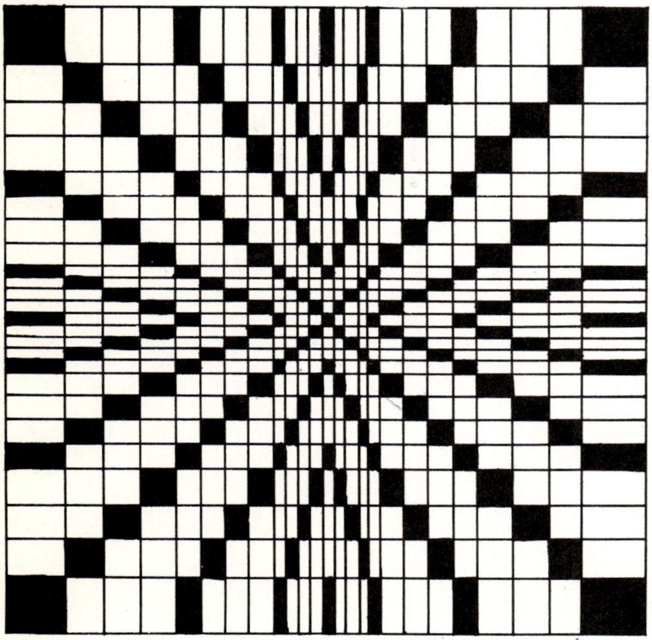

(*b*) *Straight line*

3 Blocks increasing to the centre of the unit (*123*) Woven as a cross it produces a rather concave-sided square which is difficult to use as it lacks the character of the stronger version above.

(*124*) Woven as a diamond it gives the Wheel group, and usually has the large centre block broken by stitching points. This should be woven as nearly square as possible as flattened or elongated circles always have an unpleasant appearance.

4 Blocks increasing and decreasing to the centre of the unit By combining the two previous types in one unit a strong curved chevron is woven between the arms of the cross, starting almost parallel to the edge of the square and turning to end almost perpendicular to it.

123 Running blocks increasing to centre, cross lifting

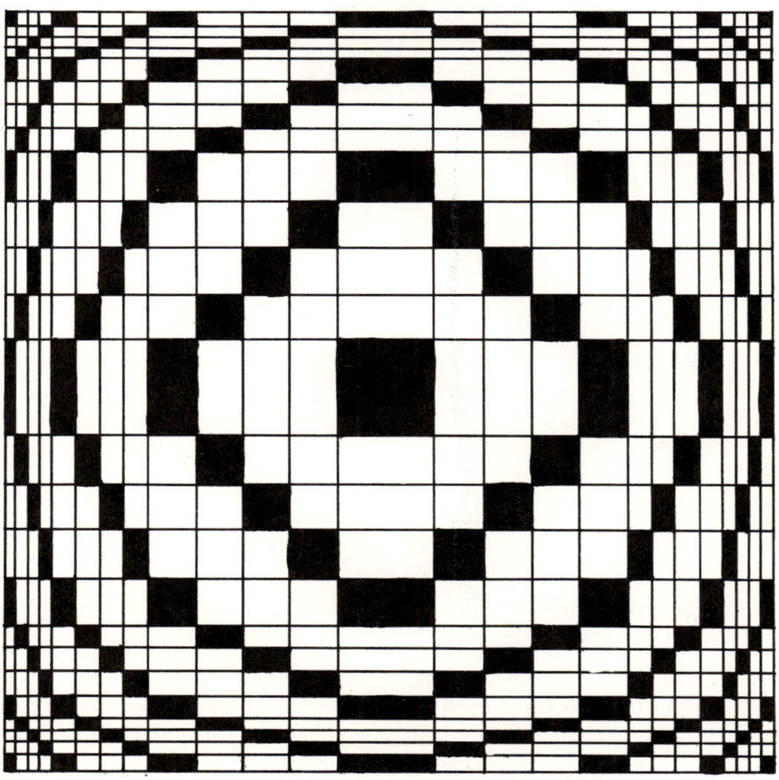

124 Running blocks increasing to centre, diamond lifting

(*125a, b*) In the smaller forms it gives a star shape, and in the larger the Bow Knot group. The block in the centre is usually broken or stitched, and the pattern can be quite small or 18 inches or more square (*134 c ii*).
(ii) *b* *Turning blocks* Turning blocks are used chiefly in two ways, to make tables at the corners of large patterns or between small units, and to weave small two-block units which combine to make larger patterns. The most popular of these are the Whig Rose-Lover's Knot patterns, using the same threading but having opposite lifting. These two-block units and tables are formed of blocks of pattern and half-tone, or in rare cases, of ground and half-tone.

125 *Running blocks increasing and decreasing to centre*
(*a*) *Star figure (diamond lifting)*

126 *Turning blocks, star lifting*

127 *Turning blocks, rose lifting*

(*126, 127*) The extreme corners of the square unit can be pattern, giving the unit a square look, or half-tone, which results in a more rounded shape as the corners appear cut off.
The former is usually called 'star', and the latter 'rose' lifting. A sequence of star units has diagonal lines running through it, and joins together; rose units do not join and do not appear continuous. The rose unit is not the back of a star unit although they both have the same threading. The star is woven as drawn in, and lifting commences with block I, while the rose starts with block II.
1 *Table, equal blocks* The design of tables is quite straight forward, the required number of threads is divided into an odd number of blocks, and each turning block itself has an odd number of ends. The two corner blocks will, of course, have an even number as they are running blocks joining the table to the rest of the design, and they should be one end more than the turning blocks to prevent them looking too small. A table can be drafted on any three adjacent shafts, and will continue into running blocks in the usual sequence. The width of the blocks in the table depends on the sett of the cloth, but is generally kept rather small to prevent it developing into an open check, which could detract from the rest of the pattern.

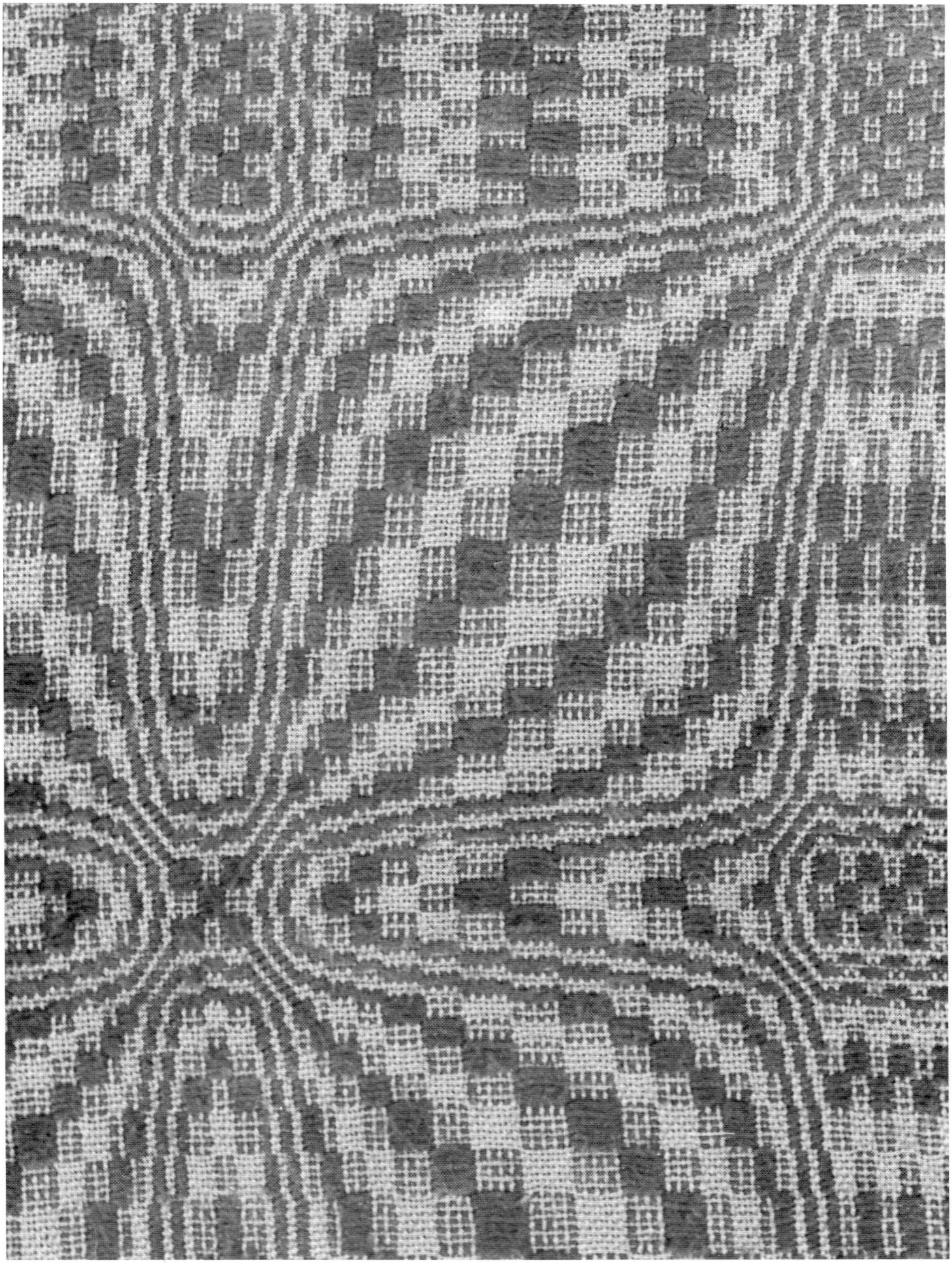

125 (b) Bow Knot figure (cross lifting)

(*128*) Tables can be split up if they become too heavy by drafting a group of ends in the centre on one of the blocks not being used for the table, being careful to maintain the sequence in the threading.

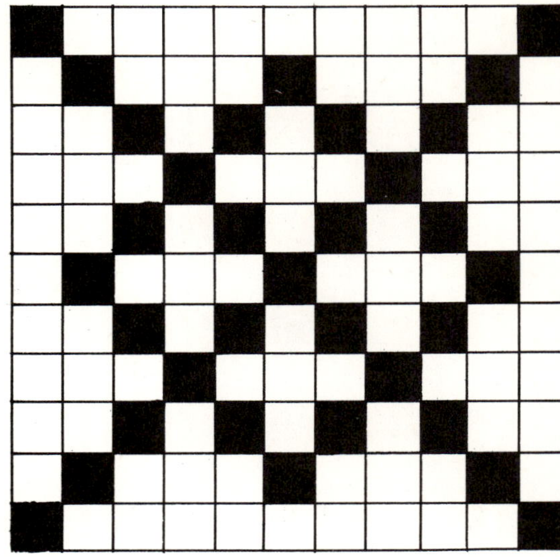

128 Split in table

(*129*) In a similar way a frame can be put round a table by returning to one of the table blocks immediately after the first block beyond the table.

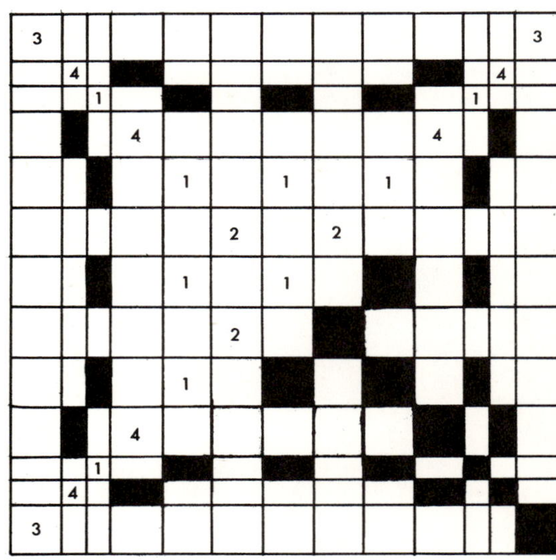

129 Frame round table

2 Star and rose figures (*130*) These designs use the same threading draft, but are lifted differently (see *126*, *127*). The complete design is formed from three two-block units for the main figure and a joining unit of running blocks. The centre unit is drafted on any pair of adjacent blocks (e.g. I and II), and the corner unit on the remaining pair (IV and III). The join is a point of four running blocks each way (I,II,III,IV,III,II,I).

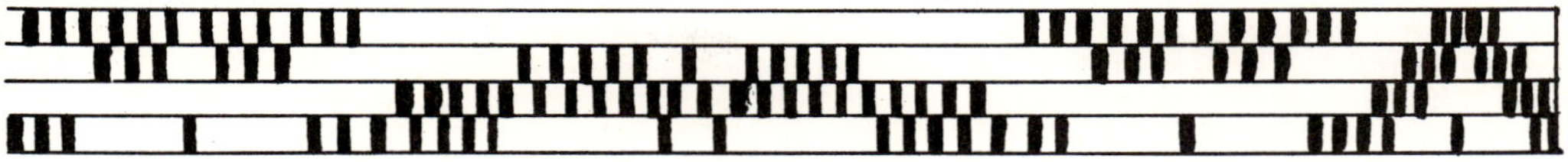

130 Star/rose draft

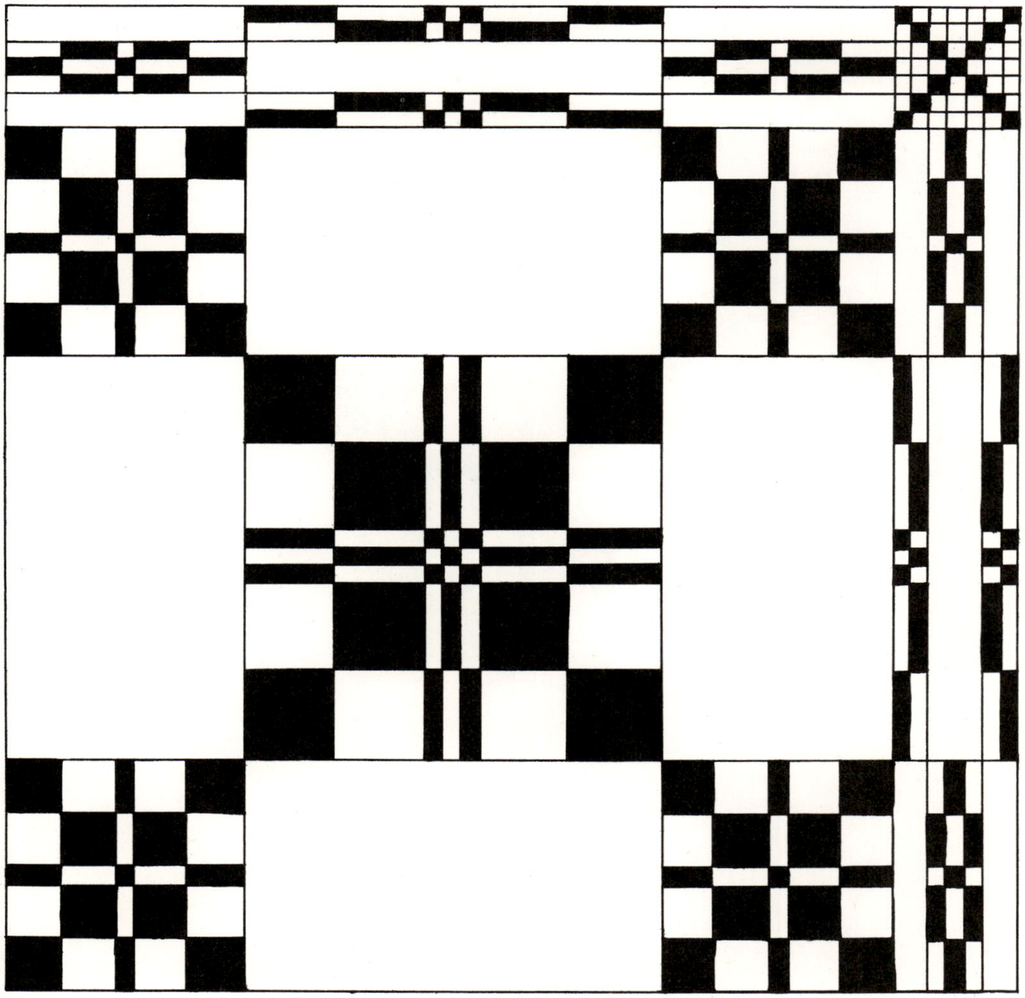

131 Star/rose block design, star lifting

(*131*) The centre unit usually has strong corners (often the first two blocks are the same size), and the centre is a compound block of three or five smaller units. A variation is to break the second block into a series of small units followed by another large block, then a final broken block in the middle.

The corner unit is similar, but smaller and less complicated, very often only five blocks, four equal and a small centre block. As the blocks must follow in sequence the centre will begin and end I,II,I,II,I,II,I, and the corner will follow IV,III,IV,III,IV, continuing with the join I,II,III,IV,III,II,I.

(*132a–c*) The join may be modified in three ways. If it is repeated as a complete unit with the centre-point one or two blocks longer than the sides two concentric circles appear round the figure (*a*), and if each arm of the join is repeated either side of the single turning-point, one double circle results (*b*). The first two and last two blocks of a join may also be doubled to thicken the circle (*c*).

132 Modified joins, block designs
(a) Join repeated as a complete unit
(b) Join extended to eight blocks

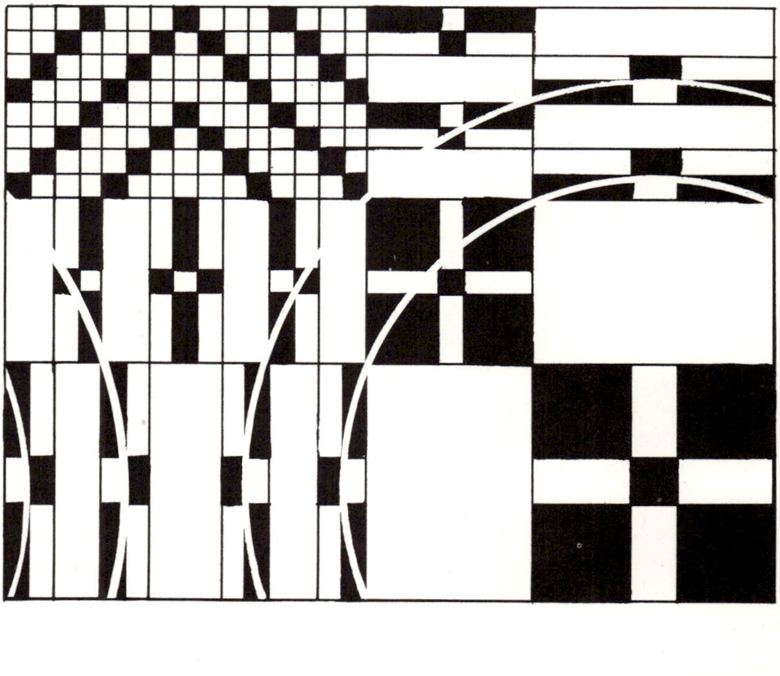

(c) Join with first two blocks doubled

3 Combined star and rose (133) Star and rose may be combined in one design by drafting the first figure as usual (I,II—II,I centre IV,III—IV corner), and the second with the blocks transposed within each figure (II,I—I,II centre and III,IV—III corner). The join is now given three sections and becomes a running unit instead of a turning unit.

133 Star and rose combined, design and block draft

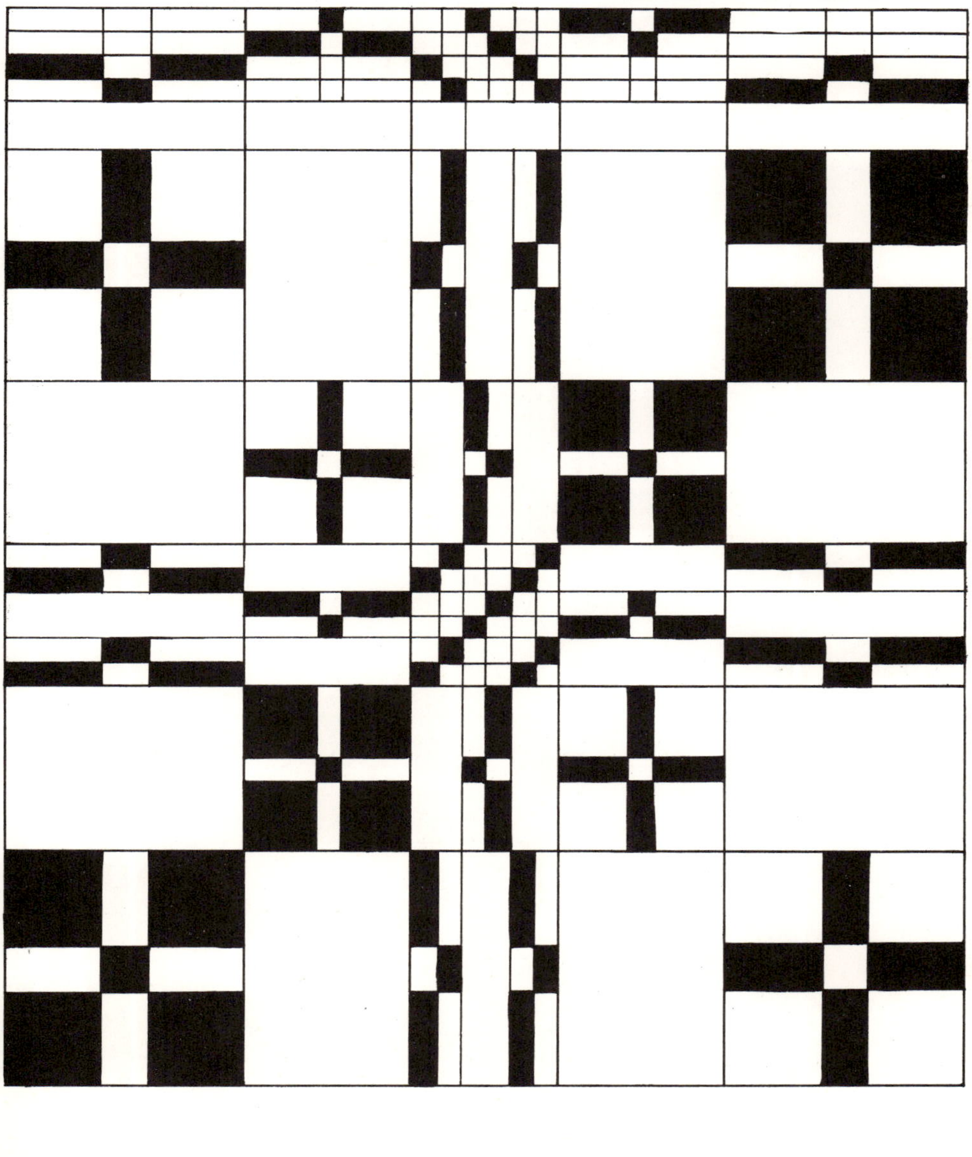

(iii) Block drafts

(*134a–c*) To save time and space an abbreviated form of drafting is often used, particularly with weaves such as Summer and Winter, double weave, damask, etc. Instead of drafting in full with each square of point paper a thread, each square now stands for a threading unit of the weave, i.e. 1,2,3,4 in double weave, 1,3,2,3 in Summer and Winter, etc.

When designing overshot patterns the relative size of the blocks is the important factor, and it is better to sketch the appearance of the design on drawing paper or point paper, and then work back to the threading, than write down a threading and then see how it weaves.

(*134a*) When designing a two-block pattern the proportions are sketched out along the top, marked on a strip of paper and placed down the side. The divisions are ruled across, and the design marked in (*i*). A block draft is next drawn out (*ii*), and for threading weaves where the length of the block is immaterial because of the structure, e.g. Summer and Winter, damask, Poor Man's Damask, double-faced twill, this is usually sufficient to thread from. (It is better to thread up thinking of the largest practicable unit, as then the chances of making mistakes are fewer. The threading draft can be written out in full if necessary.) In weaves where the length of float is limited, or the threading complicated (two-

134 Sketch block designs

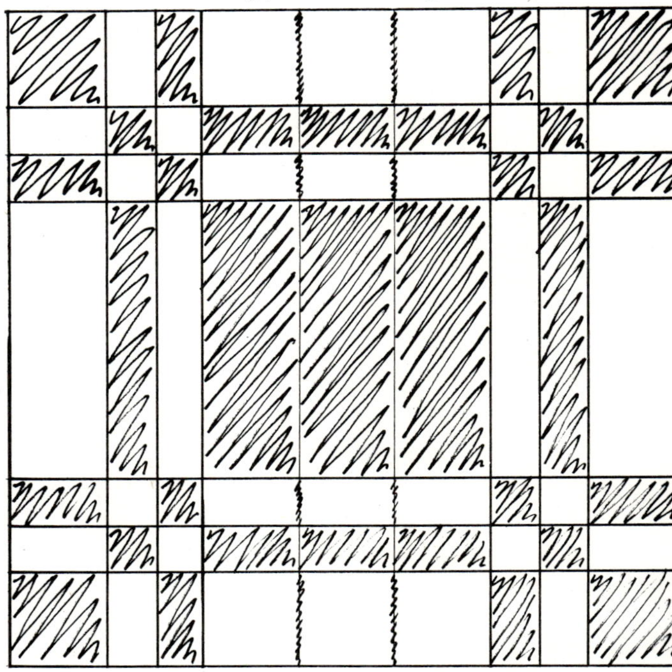

(a i) Large square block with stitching points

(a ii) Block draft

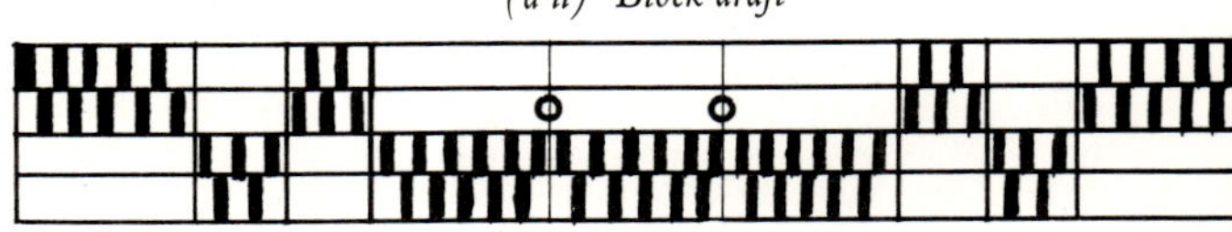

(a iii) Threading draft

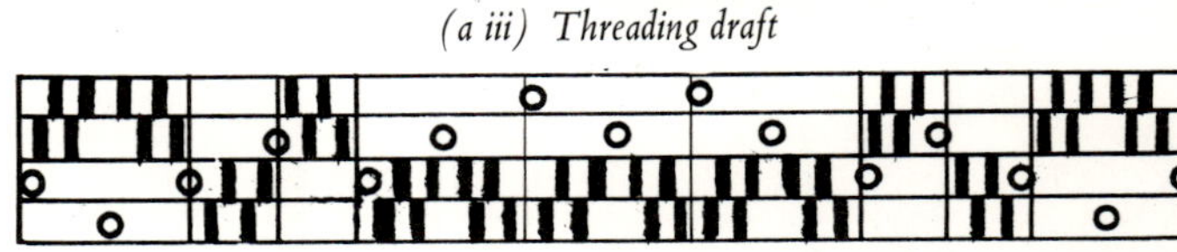

(a iv) Threading draft Poor Man's Damask (Thousand Flowers)

block overshot or some Poor Man's Damask patterns) the full threading draft is written from the block draft, adding stitching points where necessary (*iii*), ends marked 'O'. The first part of the full draft for Poor Man's Damask is given in (*iv*).

(*134b*) Four-block overshot patterns are almost invariably made up of smaller units, and these are first ruled in heavily as for the two-block patterns, followed by the subdivisions of each unit ruled in lightly in each unit. Pattern blocks are marked next in the main units, and secondary units sketched in freehand. These are the areas where the warp and weft threads of different units cross, e.g. where the weft of the centre block works through the warp of the join in (*b*) and where the weft of the figure works through the warp of the table in (*c ii*). In every case blocks on the same ends have the same width, and blocks on the same picks have the same length. Blocks of the same number form a rectangular lattice, and in patterns of running blocks particularly, one block, e.g. IV, can form a framework within which the pattern is built up (*d*), taken from (*c ii*).

All designs, from the small spot weaves to the largest overshot designs can be built up in this way. Arranging a design to fit a given number of ends is very similar to modifying designs, discussed in the next section.

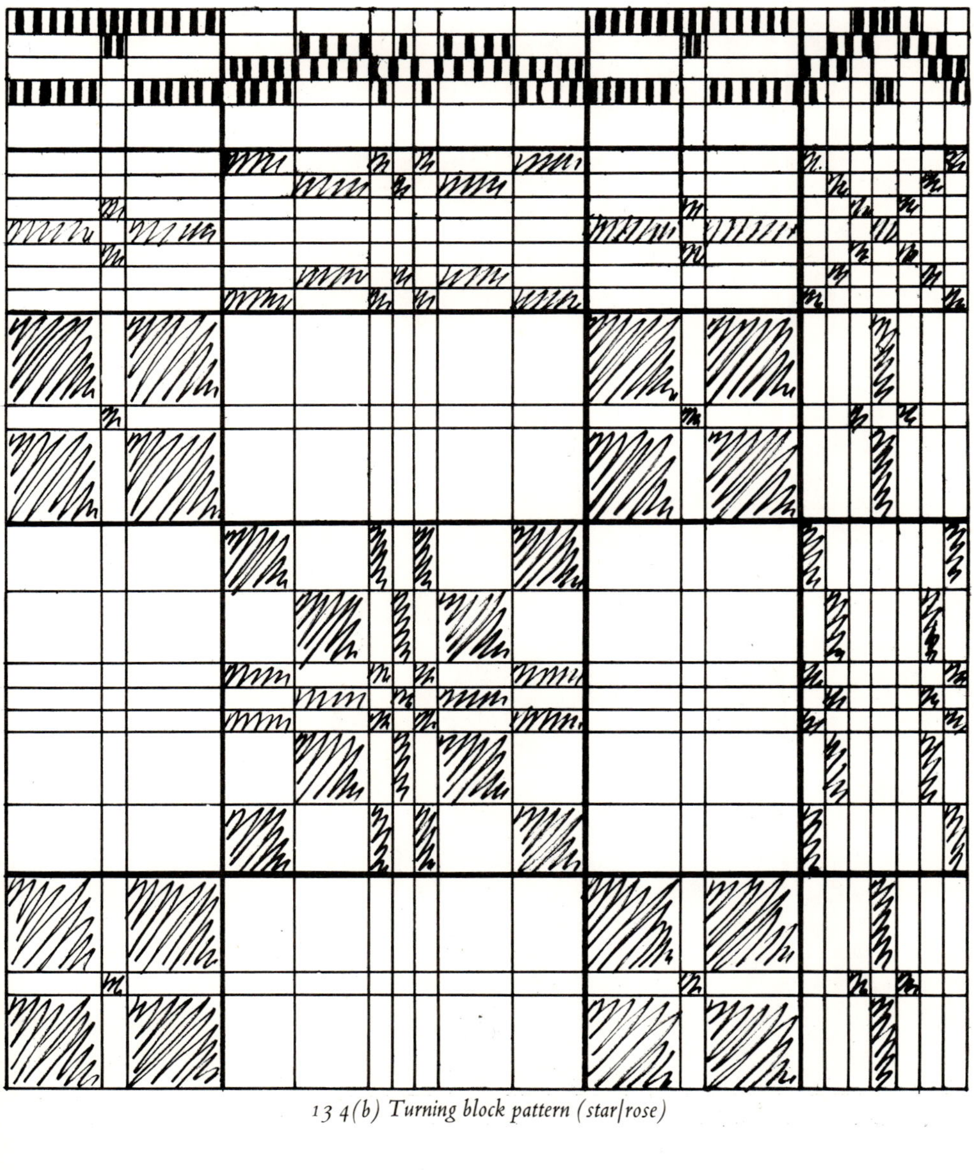

134(b) Turning block pattern (star/rose)

(iv) Modifications

It is often necessary to alter the width of a design to fit into a given number of ends, and to do it without losing the character of the original.

Firstly, the total number of threads to be added or removed is calculated and divided by the number of repeats, or halved for a single repeat. The number of blocks available over which the alteration is to be spread is compared with the number of threads. Each block can be modified only by adding or subtracting an even number of threads, otherwise running blocks become turning blocks and vice versa, or double ends

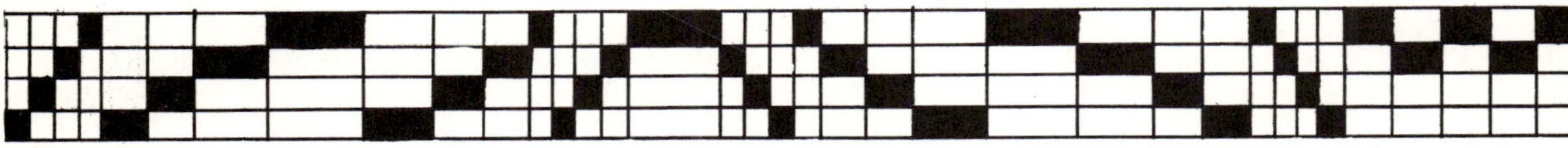

134 (c i) Bow Knot, block draft

(c ii) Bow Knot, block design

appear in the weave. The character of a figure determines where to start. If the design has heavy corners (star figures, or running blocks decreasing to the centre), additions are made to the outside blocks, and subtractions near the centre, and if the design depends on a strong centre the reverse applies.

In a table the ends are always enlarged, or the centre reduced to preserve the strength of the unit, or, if possible, two complete blocks are inserted or removed. Where the alteration is fairly small the centre of the figure can often take the whole alteration. A table centre block may be extended and then cut with a stitching unit to divide the table into four small squares, or removed altogether and the resulting double-width block treated similarly. Star and rose units are a little more difficult as the balance between centre and corner units may be lost.

In this case the same general principles apply, increasing the weight of the edge in star figures, and the centre in rose figures. This means that the same draft will be modified in two different ways, depending on the lifting. If only two ends are to be added the centre must take them, even in star figures; four ends are placed equally either side of the centre. It is sometimes better to leave the main figures alone and modify the joining unit.

Running blocks are usually easier to do as they are generally increasing or decreasing and pairs of threads can be added or subtracted where small blocks join larger ones.

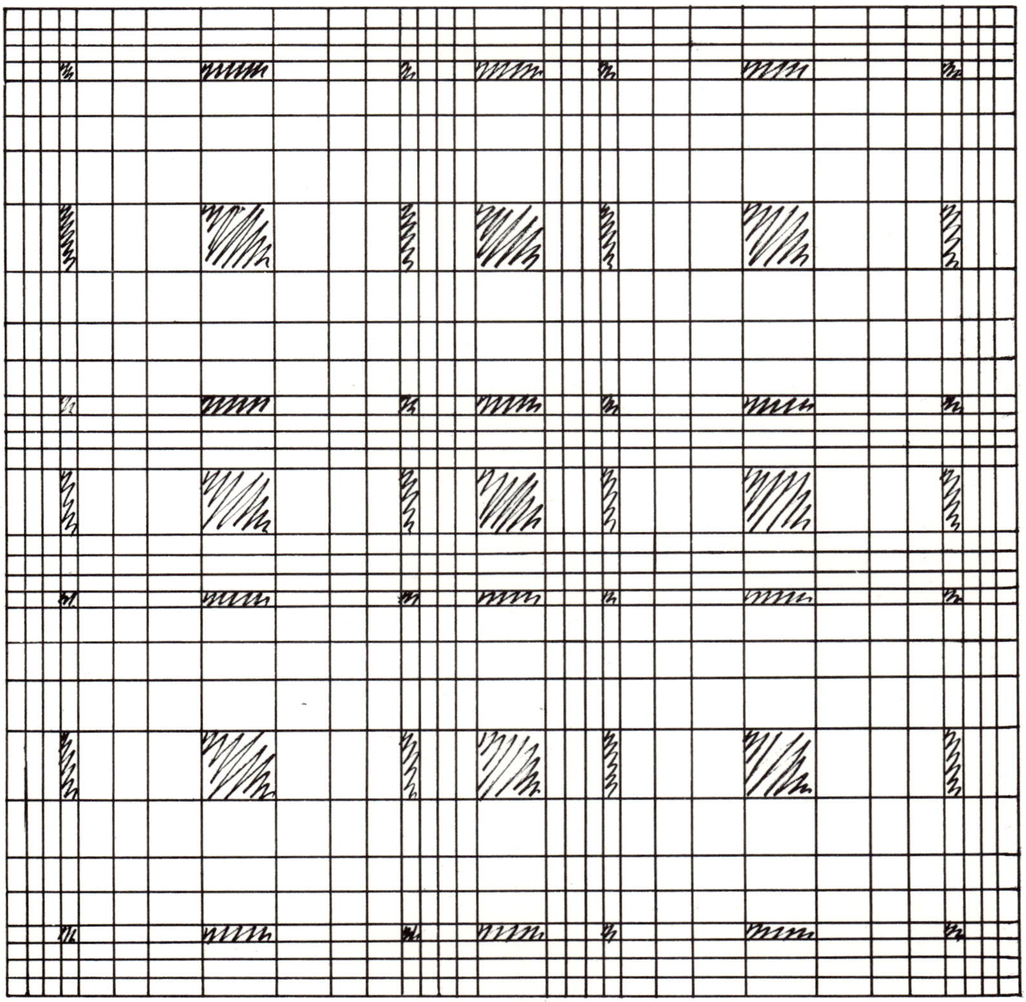

134 (d) Skeleton pattern

(*135*) If a repeating pattern is to be used on a wide warp the number of ends in one repeat is divided into the total number of ends. The width of the units of the pattern must be found, and then the number of ends required to place the first right-hand unit on the left-hand selvedge compared with the remaining number of ends. As the table units are better at the edge they can be increased or decreased to fit the width fairly easily, though if they become badly proportioned it may be necessary to alter all the similar units throughout the width of the cloth. Often a pattern will repeat a fractional number of times in width. In this case the odd fraction of the pattern is halved, and the half section used on each edge.

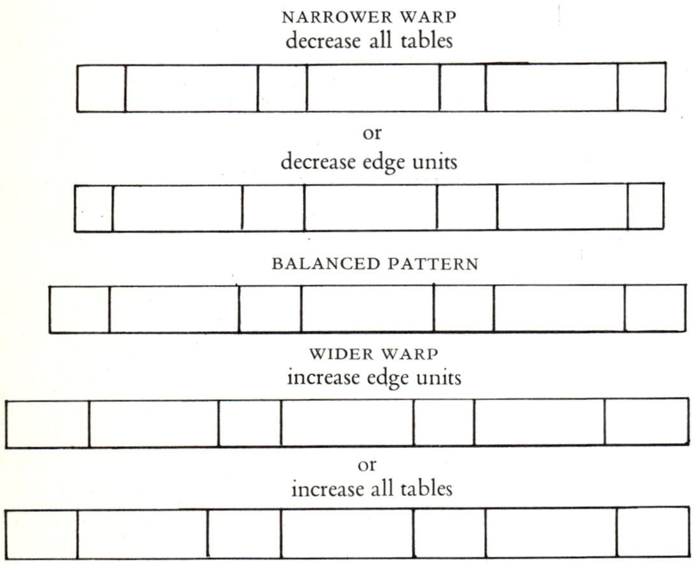

135 Block diagram of modifications of units

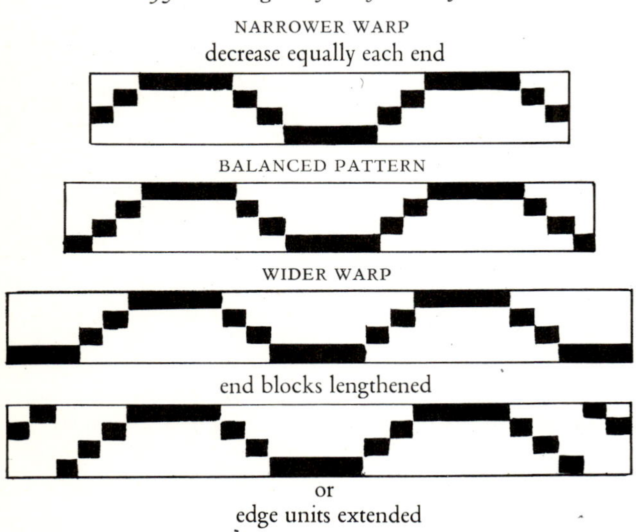

136 Block diagram of adjusting pattern to warp width

To fit Snail's Trail into a warp of 256 ends (16 in. × 16 ends per inch) (*137a-e*).
(*a*) The draft has two parts, the running unit (36 ends), and the turning unit (56 ends), totalling 92 ends.
Divide the pattern (92) into the warp (256). That gives 2 repeats (184) and 72 ends.
(*b*) Add on 1 running unit to balance the pattern (184 and 36 making 220), so 36 ends still remain.
(*c*) Add 1 more line of 4 blocks (12 ends) to each running unit. (220 and 36 making 256), *or*
(*d*) Use 3 repeats and 1 running unit. (276 and 36 making 312).
Subtract 1 line of blocks from each running unit, and 1 more block at each selvedge. (312 – 48 – 8 making 256), *or*
(*e*) Use 2 repeats and 1 *turning* unit and add 2 blocks at each selvedge. (184 and 56 making 240, and 16 making 256.)

137 Examples of modified drafts (Snail's Trail)

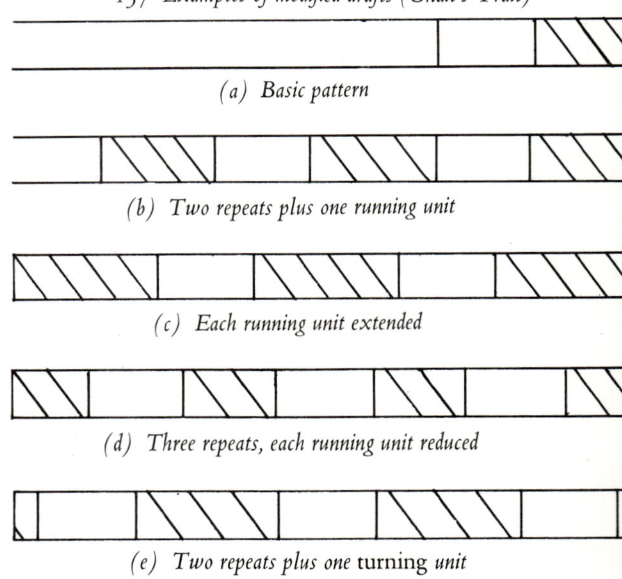

(v) Eight-shaft overshot weaves

(*138a–c, 139a, b*) The brilliant quality of drafting on opposites is used to advantage in patterns of the star and rose group (Lover's Knot, Whig Rose) by putting the weave on to eight shafts. The units are treated as two-block patterns on opposite, and are woven in pattern and ground instead of pattern and half-tone. The centre unit is placed on one-half of the harness, the front four shafts (1, 2, 3, 4), and the corner units on the back four shafts (5, 6, 7, 8). The joining unit runs across both halves of the harness. The four-shaft blocks I (1 and 2) and II (2 and 3) are now the eight-shaft

138 Eight-shaft overshot weaves

(a) Block draft

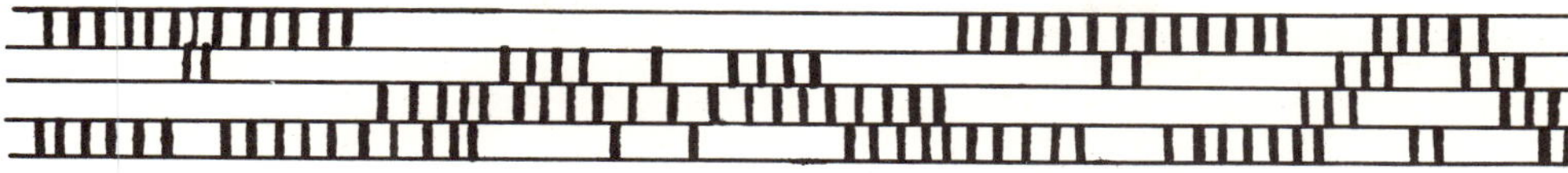

(b) Four-shaft draft

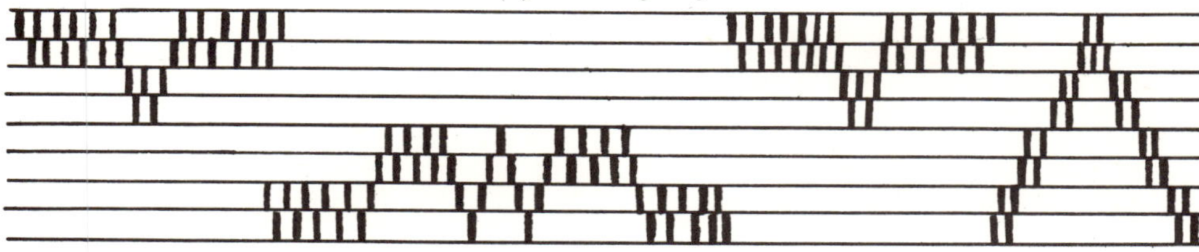

(c) Eight-shaft draft

139 Eight-shaft overshot weaves

(a) Star

(b) Rose

blocks on 1 and 2, 3 and 4, and blocks III and IV become shafts 5 and 6, 7 and 8.

While pattern is being woven on one-half of the harness, half-tone ground is woven on the other half, so the whole pattern appears on an even half-tone background instead of on a background broken up into square of half-tone and ground (*139*).

Both halves of the harness can be tied to weave half-tone at the same time, to give a cross-border to correspond roughly with a selvedge threaded straight draft across all eight shafts.

Any suitable pattern can be redrafted on eight shafts in this way by placing blocks I, II, III and IV on shafts 1 and 2, 3 and 4, 5 and 6, and 7 and 8.

B Allied weaves

(i) Summer and Winter

This is really a weave which uses a compound harness, and if this is recognised, designing in the weave is extremely simple. A compound harness has a ground and a figure harness, the former making the ground weave right across the warp, and the latter raising the blocks of the figure in the large without any ground weave.

(*140*) The ground harness in Summer and Winter is the front two shafts, on which the odd numbered ends are drawn alternately. Thus each shaft will raise every fourth end across the warp.

140 Ground harness of Summer and Winter, draft and cross-section

(*141*) The figure harness is all the rest of the shafts, the smallest number being two. The even ends are drawn on these shafts in blocks of any length, and each shaft will raise complete blocks of pattern without any weave.

141 Figure harness of Summer and Winter, draft and cross-section

(*142*) If one pattern and one ground shaft are raised together the pattern will be raised on blocks of even ends, and as every fourth end will be raised on a ground shaft the weft floats over the pattern warp are stitched down on the face of the cloth with every fourth end raised, and the floats under the warp will be stitched up by the ground shaft left down.

142 Summer and Winter, threading draft and cross-section with one ground and one figure shaft raised

(*143a–d*) Stitching shafts may be used alternately plain ground (*a*) and (*c*), or 2 and 2 Bird's Eye ground (*b*) and (*d*).

Designing is therefore simply a matter of proportion, and the abbreviated draft is used. If more than four shafts are available more pattern blocks are used on the figure harness.

(ii) Crackle weave

This is a four-block weave well known in Sweden as the 'Jämtland dräll' (i.e. Jämtland block), and called 'Crackle weave' in America by Mrs Atwater. One end in four is a stitching end, and the positioning of the stitching points and the joining of blocks follow well-defined rules.

143 *Summer and Winter*

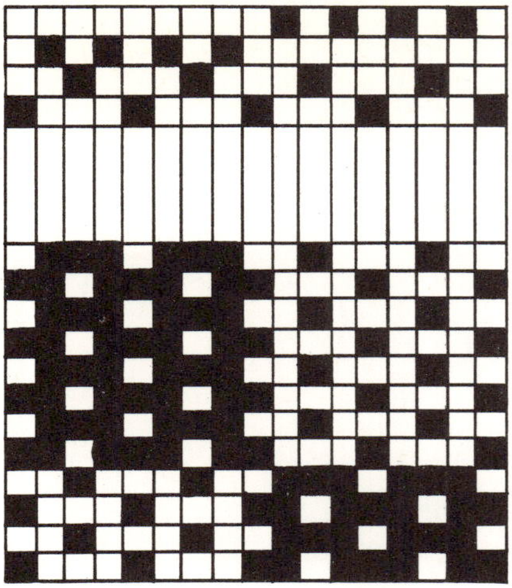

(a) Plain ground, block diagram

(c) Plain ground, cloth

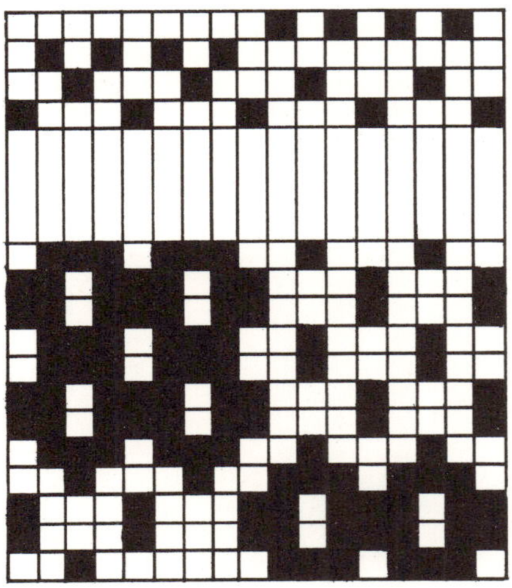

(b) Bird's Eye ground, block diagram

(d) Bird's Eye ground, cloth

(144) This shows all four blocks drafted as a small running pattern. Block I is centred on shaft 1 and runs 4,1,2,1; block II is centred on shaft 2 and runs 2,3,2,1; block III is 2,3,4,3, and block IV is 4,1,4,3. The joins follow the rule that each block begins, with or without a stitching end, exactly as the previous one finished, i.e. both or neither having stitching ends. When drafting the threading for a pattern the stitching end to start with is on the shaft *behind* the shaft carrying the block, i.e. if the block shafts are running 1,2,3,4, the stitching shafts will be 4,1,2,3, respectively. If the draft continues running this order will be maintained. At turning-points the

144 *Crackle weave draft (Jämtland dräll)*
(a) Running blocks
(b) Draft with turning-points

(a)

(b)

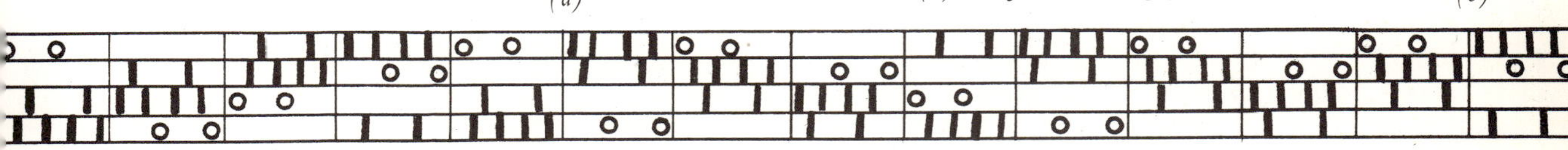

order automatically rearranges itself at the first join without stitching ends after the turning block, when block and stitching shafts change places (joins (*a*) and (*b*)). Blocks may be any width from one unit upwards, and two, three or four blocks may equally well be used. Three is drafted as for four blocks, but two blocks are usually drafted on opposites, with an extra end between the blocks at the joins, which otherwise obey the normal sequence (*145*).

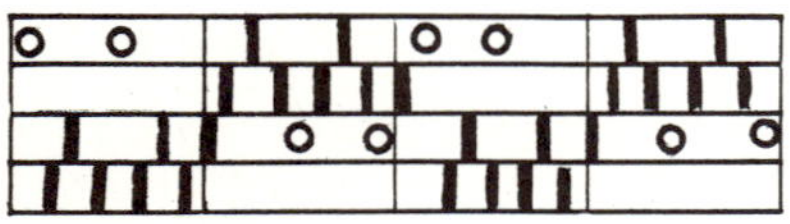

145 Crackle weave, two-block

The lifting is the same as for any other block (overshot) weave, block I is 1 and 2, II is 2 and 3, III is 3 and 4, IV is 4 and 1, and plain weave is 1 and 3, 2 and 4. Each block overlaps the one on each side, so there is no ground as in the ordinary four-block overshot weave, the half-tone covering all the space between the pattern blocks (*146*).

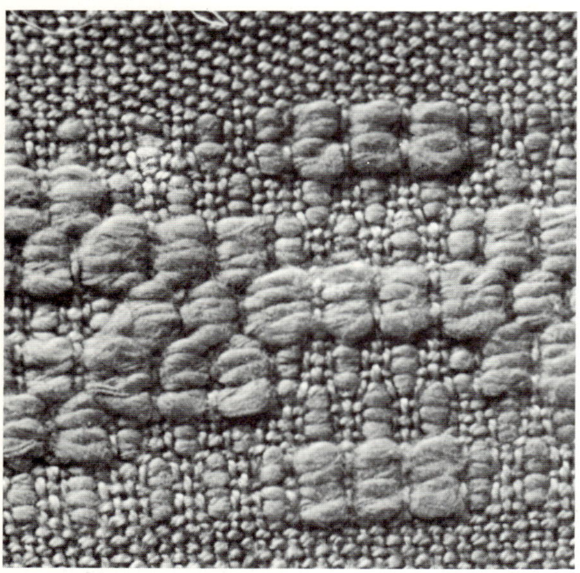

146 Crackle weave, two-block

(iii) Poor Man's Damask

(*147a, b*) This is a useful two-block weave in which the pattern weft is stitched on every fifth end. Though superficially similar to Summer and Winter weave, the construction is entirely different. It is really a two-block pattern on opposites, usually 1 and 2, 3 and 4, with stitching points taken out in sequence. (*a*) shows the basic draft, (*b*) the complete draft with stitching ends taken out of the plain weave. A stitching end always separates the blocks. Lifting is as for the two-block overshot patterns 1 and 2, 3 and 4 for pattern, and 1 and 3, 2 and 4 for plain weave.

147 Poor Man's Damask

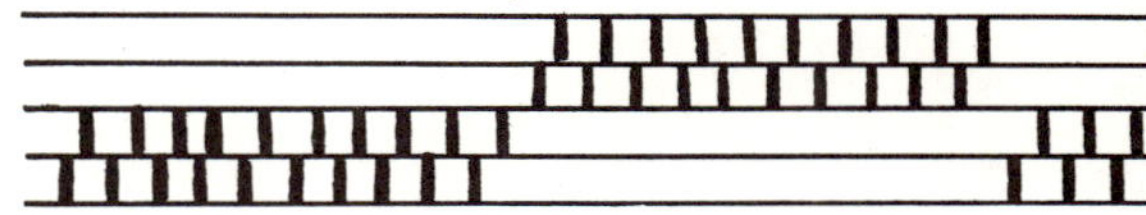

(a) Two-block design on opposites

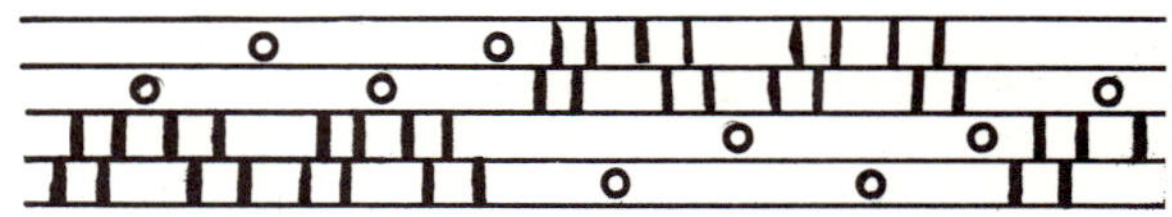

(b) Two-block design on opposites, with stitching points

6 Textured weaves

This group includes for convenience the weaves which give an all-over cellular texture with a simple weave. The true cellular gauze and leno weaves are dealt with in chapter 9.

(i) All-over texture

(i) *a Huckaback* (*148a, b*) This cloth is used primarily for towels, and is based on the plain weave for firmness, but has comparatively long floats to absorb moisture. The draft is simple, (*a*) is a slightly better version as the centre shafts are less crowded with heddles; (*b*) is a continuous running threading and avoids jumping from back to front at each repeat, which can be a cause of threading mistakes.

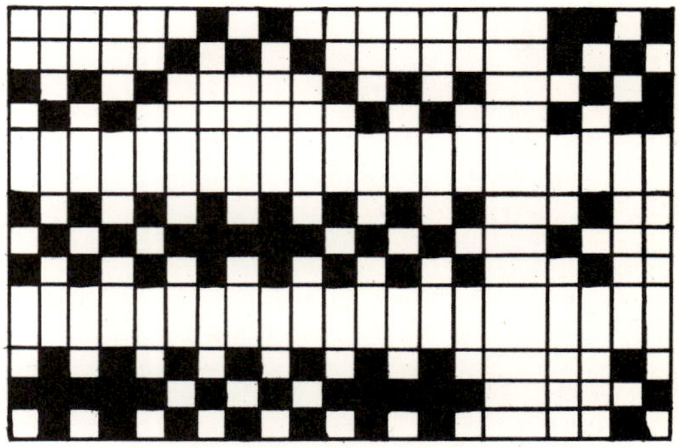

(b) Alternative draft

(*149*) is the commercial threading, and has the advantage of converting easily to plain weave by tying the front and back pairs of shafts together for plain weave, using two treadles, two lamms, and only the top pulleys on a counter-balanced loom.

148 Huckaback drafts

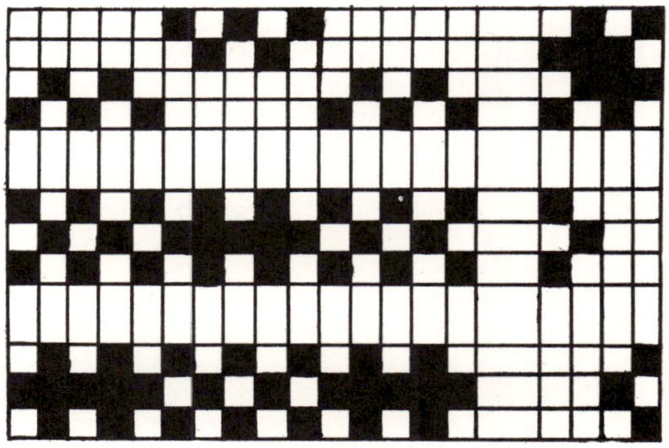

(a) Alternative draft

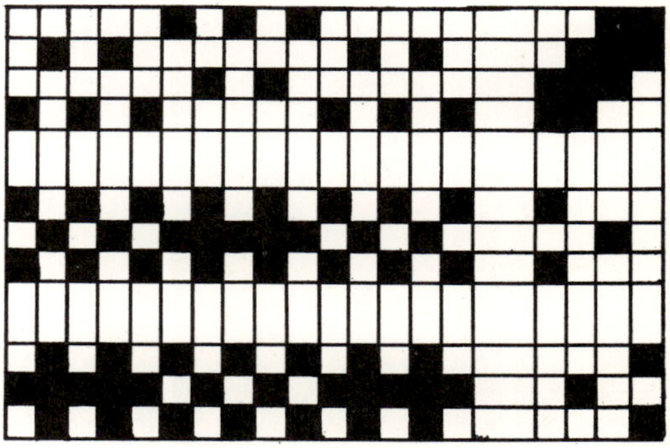

149 Commercial huckaback

(*150a, b*) The weave can be extended warp way and weft way by adding pairs of ends to each block, or weaving two more picks. It is often woven with five ends and three picks, as well as five ends and five picks.

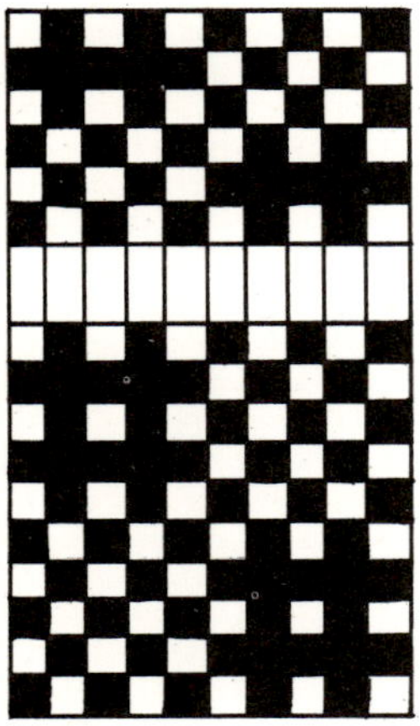

150 *Huckaback weave plans (lifting as weave plan)*
(a) Five ends, three picks
(b) Five ends, five picks

(*151*) In a reversible version rows of warp and weft flush units alternate.
As all the five ends in one unit tend to run together they are sleyed with the last end of one unit and the first of the next in the same dent of the reed, and the middle three ends together in the following dent.

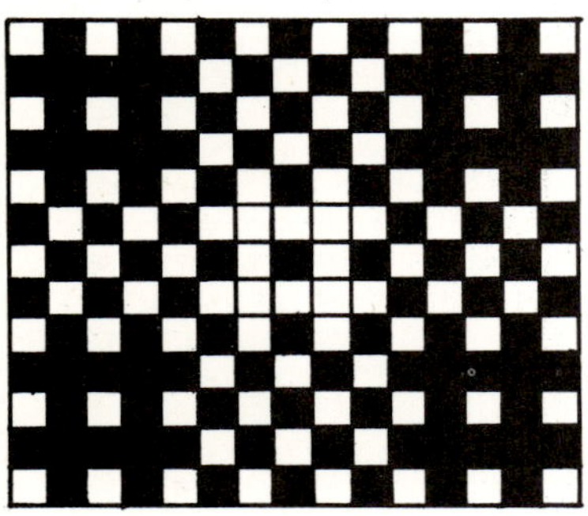

151 *Reversible huckaback, 5 × 5, lifting as weave plan*

(i) *b Canvas weave* This is an imitation gauze weave used, among other things, for embroidery canvas. In finer yarns it is useful for net curtains, light dress fabrics, blouse fabrics, etc., often in combination with other weaves.

(*152a, b*) The draft is the same as the huckaback, but the lifting gives alternating warp and weft units in both directions, and no plain weave (*a*). If possible a reed of a sett coarse enough to take all five ends of a unit should be employed, and for a pronounced openwork effect a finer sett with alternate dents missed between the units (*b*).

152 *Canvas weave*

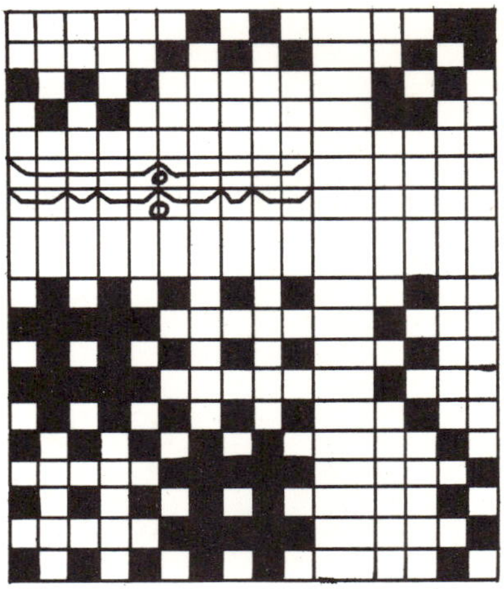

(a) Weave plan

(b) Cloth

(*153*) The weave may be modified by omitting the centre end and pick, allowing the second and fourth ends and picks to run together. These ends can be somewhat thicker to give a coarse weave effect bound together by the finer first and last threads.

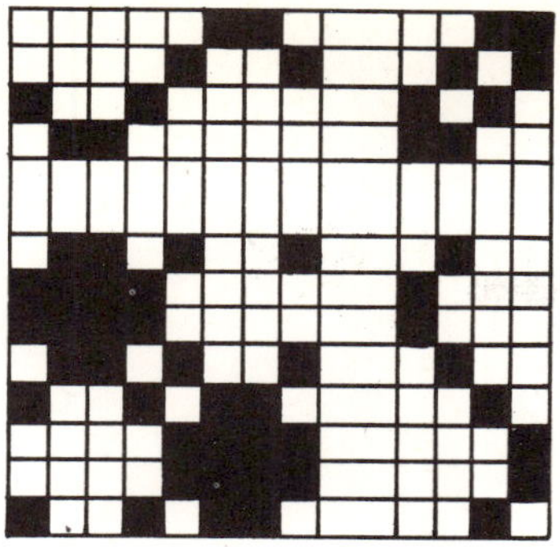

153 *Modified canvas weave*

(i) *c Mock leno* (154*a*, *b*) Although this is really a group of weaves in which the canvas weave (*b*) can be included, the name, for handweavers at least, is generally applied to the weave in which the same unit as the canvas weave alternates with one single end, giving a warp-faced fabric. This unit can be three, five or seven ends wide, and is usually woven square.

154 *Mock leno weave*

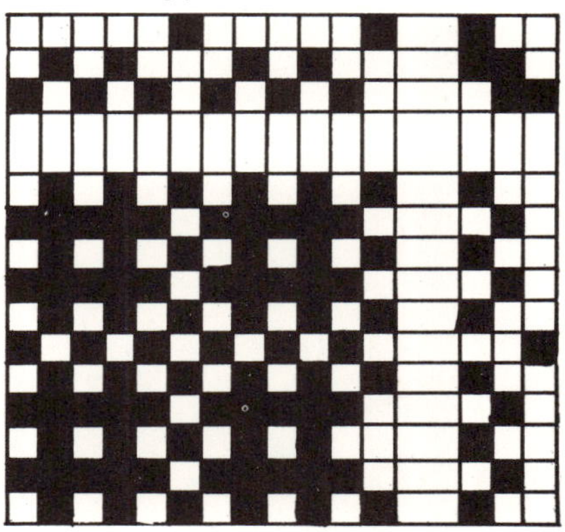

(*a*) *Weave plan*

(*b*) *Cloth*

(i) *d Honeycomb* The honeycomb weave is a fairly loose one, and the variety of interlacing and therefore of the tension in individual threads causes them to move considerably in the finishing, throwing the fabric into a series of ridges and hollows warp way and weft way. (155) shows a cross-section through the cloth, and (156*a*–*c*) the threading, lifting and weaving plan. The lifting may be as (*a*), which is the usual way, and gives weft floats two threads shorter than the warp floats but a more regular construction, while (*b*) gives an equal length of float both ways by adding two more picks in the centre. The floats along the tops of the ridges are indicated on the weave plan.

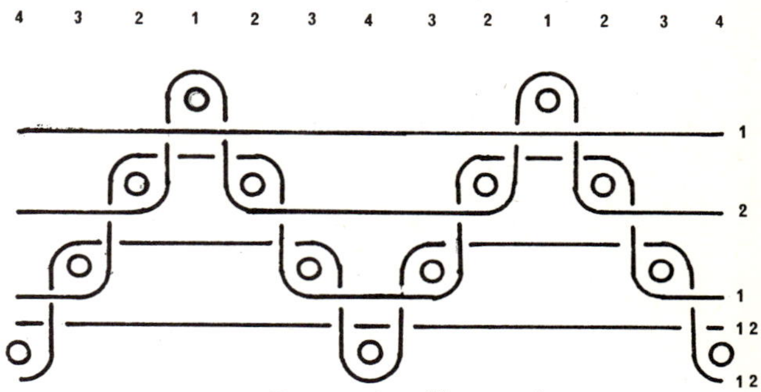

155 *Cross-section of honeycomb*

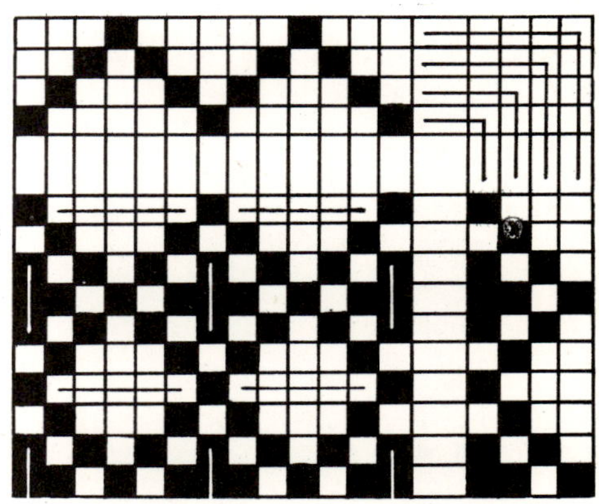

156 *Honeycomb* (*a*) *Standard weave*

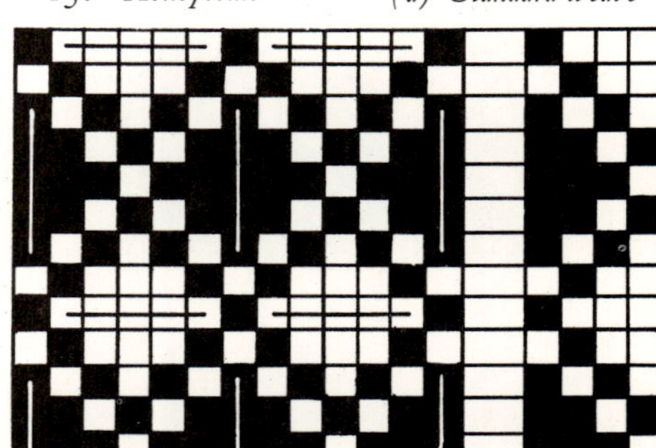

(*b*) *Standard weave, with extra picks added in centre*

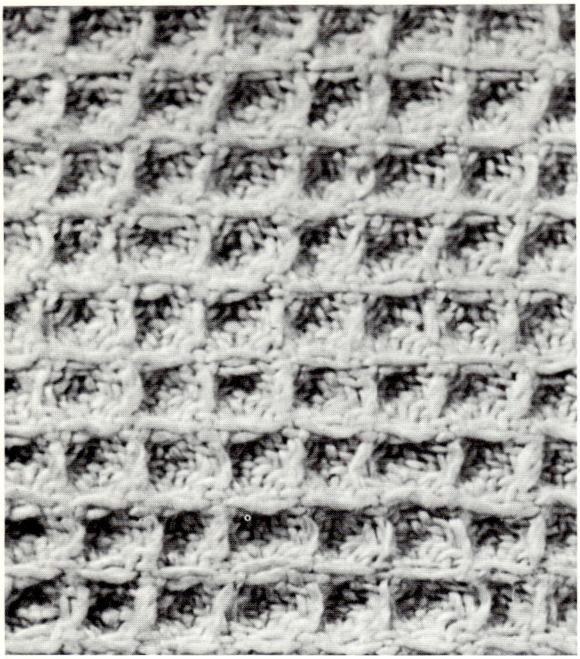

156 *(c) Cloth*

The general rule for all simple honeycombs is to use a point draft threading. For the lifting plan place a row of marks diagonally from the top left to the bottom right corners, leave one row of blanks, and fill in the whole of the rest of the lower left corner. The upper right corner is left blank (*156a*). An extra pick can be added below the lower left corner, extending across all the shafts except the last (*156b*). The lifting plan is, of course, reversed to complete the repeat.

An interesting variation is the Brighton Honeycomb, which needs a multiple of four ends and picks.

157 *Brighton honeycomb*

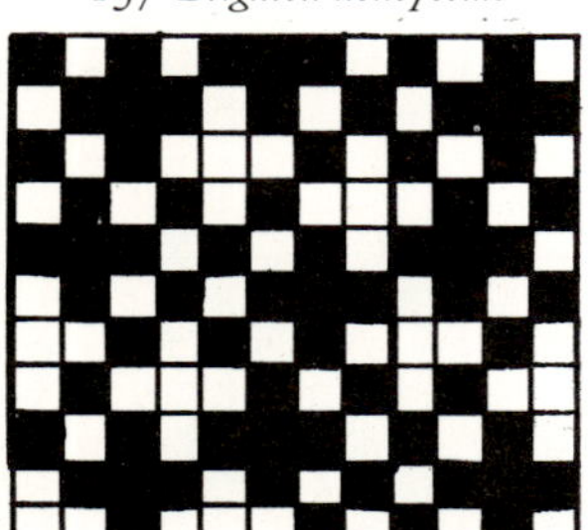

(a) Eight-end, lifting as weave plan

The smallest, (*157*), is complete on eight ends and picks. The lifting plan is the same as the weave plan with a straight draft.

(b) Sixteen end, lifting as weave plan

(c) Cloth

(ii) Two-block and stripe weaves

The mock leno weave can be used for two-block patterns, an openwork block alternating with a plain weave block. This is often called 'Swedish Lace', a term which also covers a group of patterns based on a spot weave, with a plain shaft and several spotting shafts, and which has lines of running units and tables; (see Weaves based on plain cloth, chapter 4, section (i)). This second type of Swedish Lace is in the group which includes both types of the 'Bronson' weave, one version of which is also called 'Barley-corn'.

The difficulties caused by the confused terminology can be resolved by going back to the fundamentals. The

Barley-corn, both Bronsons, and the Swedish Lace weaves are all spot weaves which have one plain shaft, several spotting shafts, and may or may not have a ground shaft behind the plain shaft.

The canvas and huckaback weaves cannot be used for two-block patterns on four shafts, but can be used for stripes of pattern and plain weave provided allowance is made for the difference in warp take-up (e.g. two warp rollers or one roller and weighted rods). If two-block patterns are needed the simplest way is to place the alternate blocks on the front and back halves of an eight-shaft harness.

The two-block and the stripe four-shaft weaves are all reducible to threadings with either a plain and a ground shaft and two spotting shafts, or with the plain and ground shafts combined to form a pair of split plain shafts with two spotting shafts. These weaves are drafted in many different ways, which tends to conceal the group from which any specific weave has come, but if the weaves are rearranged to bring the plain and ground shafts or the split plain shafts to the front the grouping immediately becomes apparent.

(*158a–b*) This common version of a two-block mock leno is fairly easy to recognise (*a*). Shaft 2 is brought to the front, and shaft 1 is taken back in its place, to give a weave with a plain and a ground shaft and two spotting shafts (*b*).

158 *Two-block mock leno*

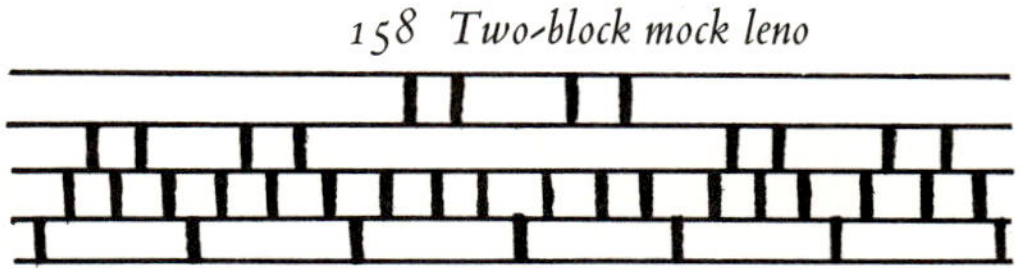

(*a*) *Standard draft*

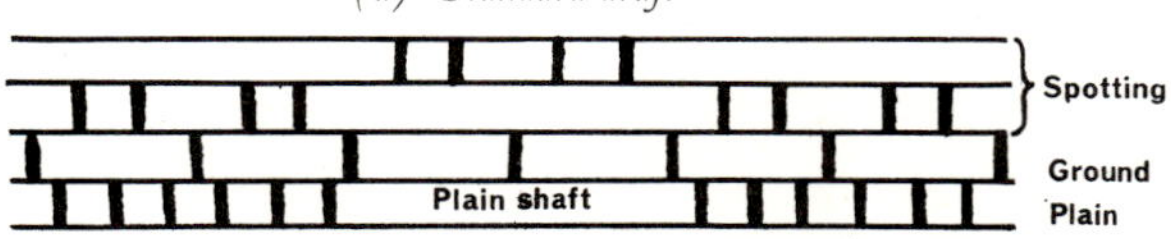

(*b*) *Reduced to plain ground and spotting shafts*

(*c*) *Weave plan*

(*159a, b*) In this threading shaft 3 is the ground, and is brought to shaft 2, and shaft 2 taken back to become shaft 3, (*a*), giving the same type of threading as before in (*158b*), but with single spots (*b*).

159 *Two-block Bronson weave*

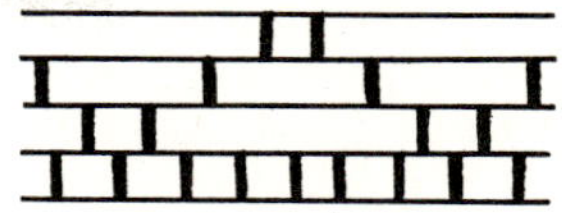

(*a*) *Standard draft*

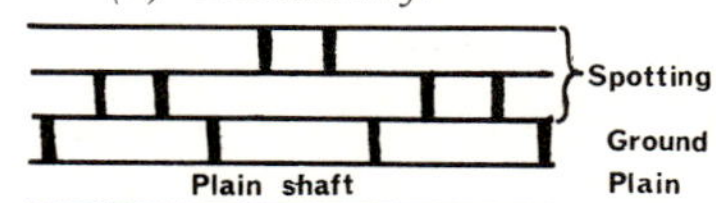

(*b*) *Reduced to plain ground and spotting shafts*

(*160a–d*) In these two variations of spot (Bronson) weave, the shafts 2 and 3 are transposed as in (*159*), becoming (*160b, d*) respectively, with plain and ground shafts and two spotting shafts, (*b*) having a stitching end between adjacent spots, and (*d*) without stitching but with opposite spots.

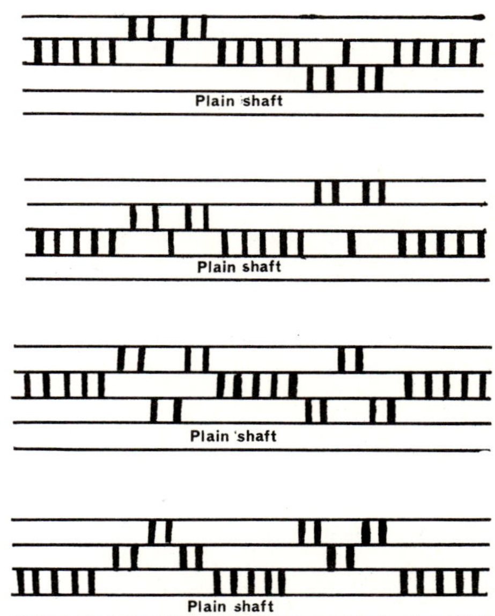

160 *Two variations of spot weaves*
(*a*) (*c*) *Standard drafts*
(*b*) (*d*) *Reduced drafts*

(*161a, b*) is a standard two-block mock leno draft, and in (*b*) is rearranged with a pair of split plain shafts and two spotting shafts, to show the similarity between this and the draft in (*158*). The spotting shafts are the same, but by combining the plain and ground shafts, and then redividing them as a pair of split plain shafts a more balanced draft is obtained, particularly for a loom with a counter-balanced harness. There would, of course, be no practical advantage in using the rearranged draft of (*161b*) for weaving in this particular case; it has been done merely to demonstrate the principle involved.

(*162a*) shows a standard canvas weave and/or huckaback threading similarly arranged in (*162b*), and in all three cases a plain weave stripe would be threaded alternately on the split plain shafts (1 and 4 in *161a*; 1 and 2 in *161b*, *162b*; 2 and 3 in *162a*.

161 Mock leno weave

(a) Standard draft

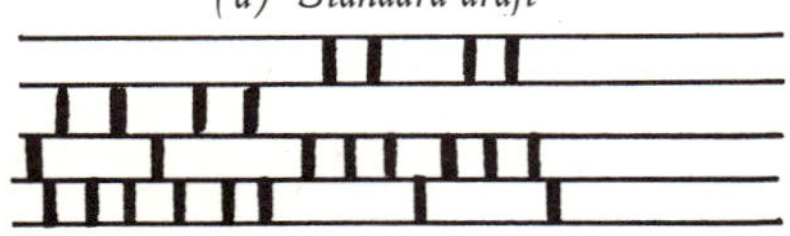

(b) Reduced to split plain and two spotting shafts

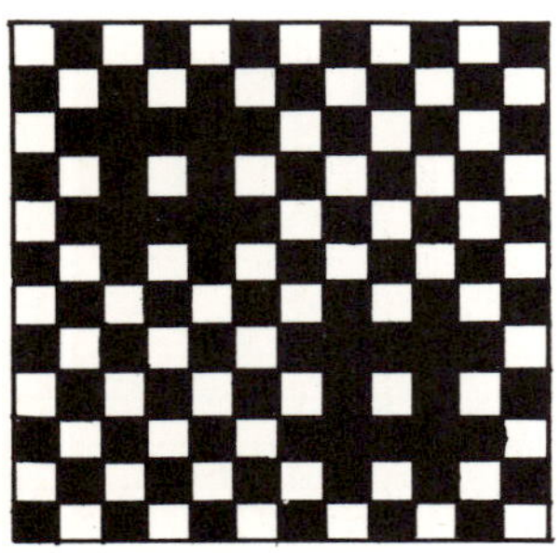

(c) Weave plan

162 Canvas and huckaback weaves

(a) Standard

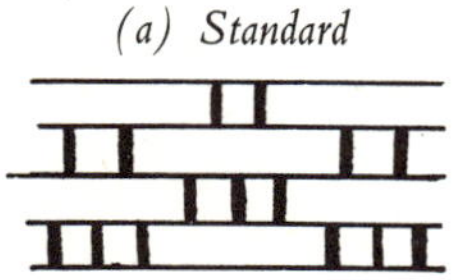

(b) Reduced to split plain and two spotting shafts

(ii) *a* *Mock leno patterns (two-block)* (*163a–c*) give the two standard threadings for the two-block mock leno. Blocks are designed in units of six ends, but if thick or thin yarns are used the units can be decreased to four ends or increased to eight ends. The total number of ends in a block is one less than the number of units multiplied by six, as the single end of the final unit of one block is the first end of the unit at the beginning of the next block. Plain weave stripes are invariably threaded alternately on the shafts which carry the majority of the ends in one unit, and the single ends of the other unit, i.e. the split plain shafts. The Swedish Lace version of the threading (*158b*) has blocks an exact number of units wide, as the final stitching end is not part of the first opposite unit, and is easily expansible into three or more blocks by using more shafts. Both versions can be woven with either block, both blocks together (*163c*), or with a border of plain weave.

163 Two-block mock leno, standard threading
(a) (b) Alternative threadings

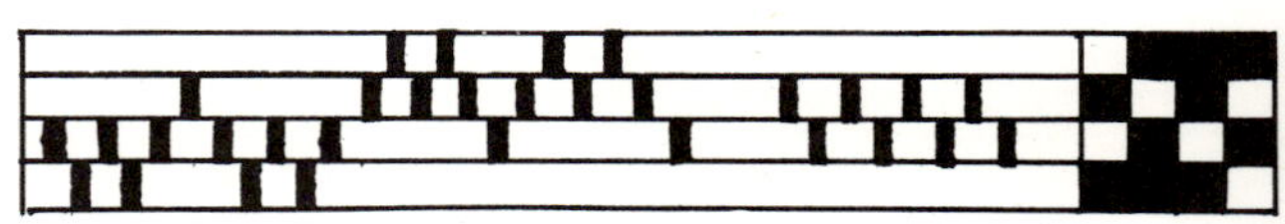

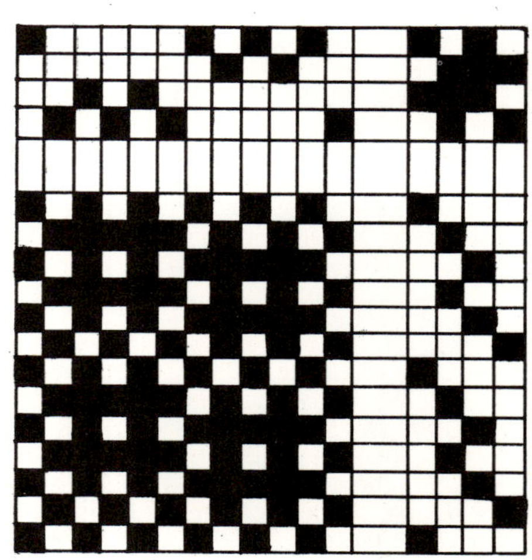

(c) Weave diagram with both blocks weaving pattern together

(ii) *b Canvas weave patterns (stripes) (164)* This, like the mock leno can be drafted with the majority of the ends on the outer or inner pair of shafts (*148a, b*). If a high sett is used the outer shafts should carry the greater number of ends to work more easily (*148a*), but the threading runs more smoothly without jumping, and therefore with the chance of fewer errors the other way round (*148b*). Units may have three ends and three picks (ordinary point threading), five ends and five picks, etc. The plain weave stripe is on the split plain shafts.

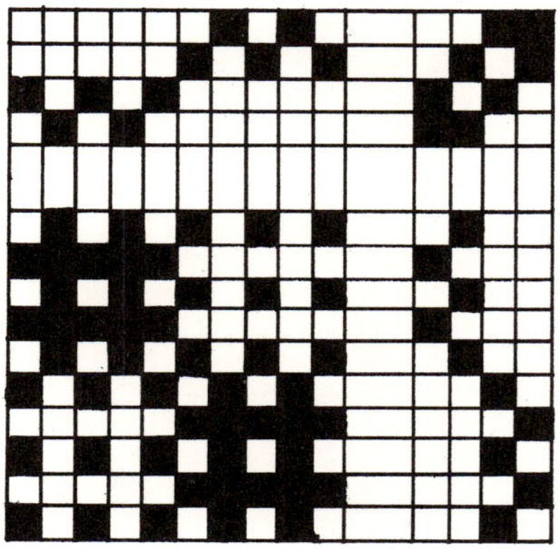

164 Canvas weave diagram

(ii) *c Huckaback (stripes) (165)* The only difference between this and the canvas weave is the extra end raised on picks 2 and 4 of each unit. Otherwise the whole of section (ii) *b* (canvas weave) applies to huckaback. Units need not be balanced in the huckaback weaves, but may be five ends and three picks, seven ends and five picks, seven ends and three picks, etc.

165 Huckaback

(a) Block I

(b) Block II

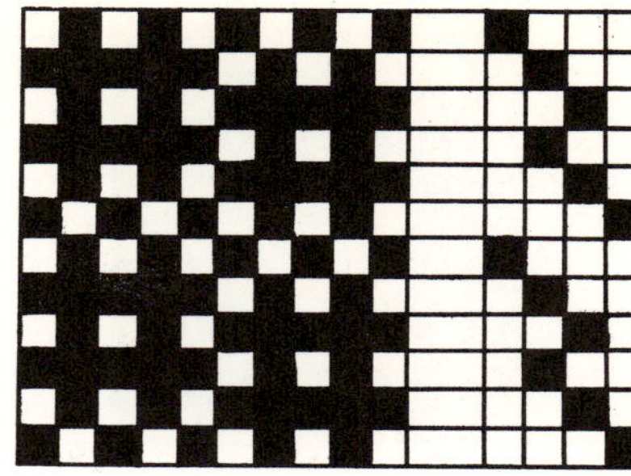

(c) Blocks I and II

(ii) *d Ms and Os (166a, b)* This gives alternate blocks of $\frac{4}{4}$ weft rib weave and plain weave. As the weft rib is a looser weave the plain weave expands in the finishing and compresses the rib so that the sides of the blocks are curved.

166 Ms and Os

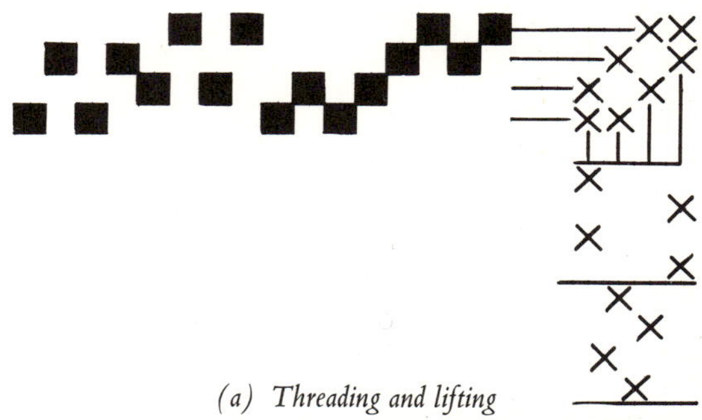

(a) Threading and lifting

(b) Cloth with fancy yarns

(*167a, b*) A three-block version can be woven by using the third pair of shafts (inside, 2 and 3, and outside, 4 and 1) for the third block, but slight faults appear in the plain weave. Both the two- and three-block patterns can be woven with a $\frac{5}{5}$ rib, with an odd number of ends per block.

167 Ms and Os, three-block

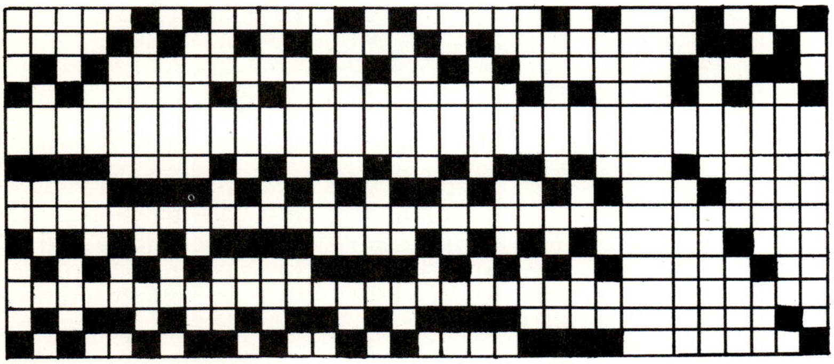

(a) Weave diagram with an even number of ends per block

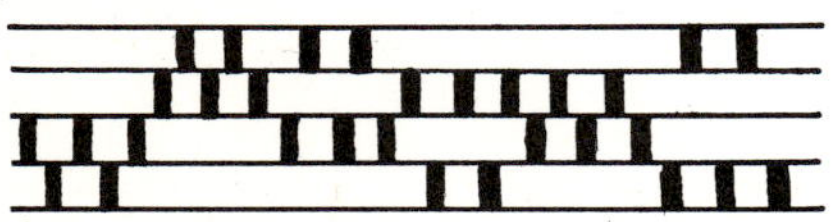

(b) Threading draft with an odd number of ends per block

(*168*) A five-shaft version with three blocks.

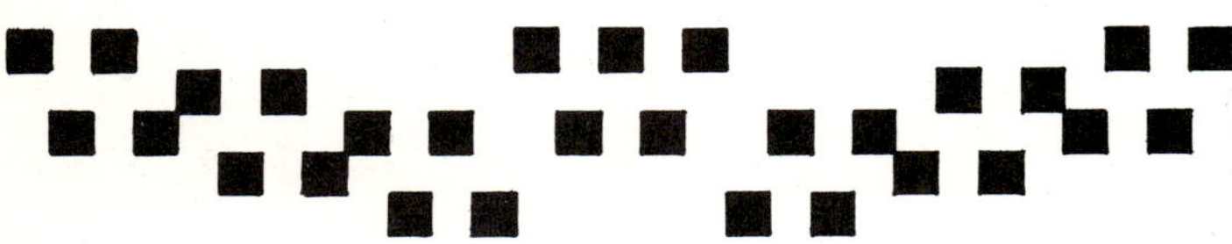

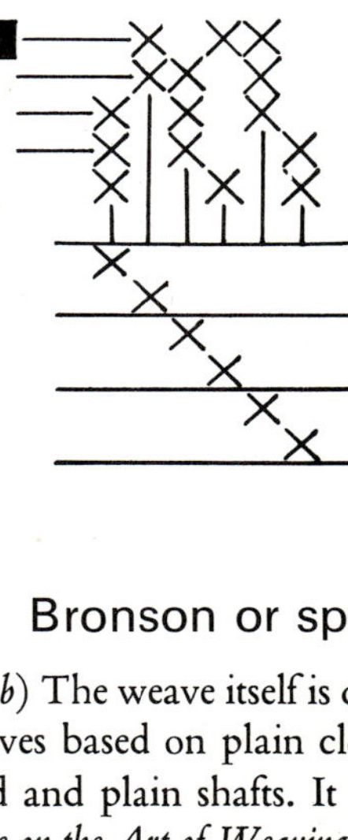

168 Modified five-shaft Ms and Os

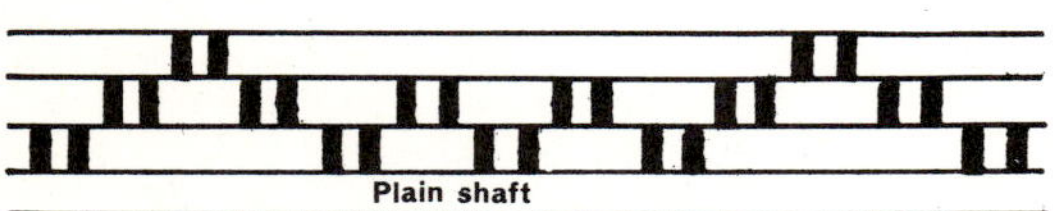

169 Spot weave with (a) one plain and three spotting shafts

'The following is a plan of an allover spot mounting, with a double draught, the pattern of which may be easily traced on design paper, by making the spot treading follow the same order as the draught on the leaves.'

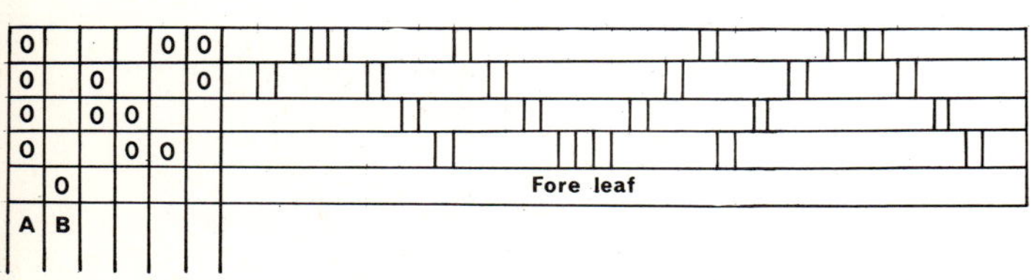

(b) one plain and four spotting shafts (redrawn from John Murphy's Treatise*)*

(iii) Bronson or spot weave

(*169a, b*) The weave itself is discussed under the heading of weaves based on plain cloth with a ground shaft or ground and plain shafts. It appears in John Murphy's *Treatise on the Art of Weaving* as a spotting weave, and in the Bronson brothers' book as a diaper. It is also known as 'Barley-corn' in Europe. It is generally drafted with one plain shaft and three spotting shafts for a four-shaft mounting (*a*), though the old drafts seem to use at least a five-shaft mounting, giving four spotting shafts (*b*). Tables are drafted on alternate blocks of two adjacent shafts.

(iv) Pile weaves

(iv) *a* *Warp pile* (*170*) Velvet is a true warp pile cloth. It needs two warps, a ground warp which, with the weft, makes a firm back in plain weave or a three- or four-end twill, and a pile warp which weaves into the ground and is cut after weaving to make the pile. The pile warp weaves into the ground for an odd number of picks (three in *170*), and is then raised over a rod which goes between the pile and ground warps. The shed is closed and the pile warp works through the ground again. This is repeated several times, and then the first rod inserted is taken out and used again. This continues for the length of the warp. On a proper velvet loom the rods are polished brass with a small groove along the top, and an extremely sharp knife is slid along the groove to cut the rod free and leave the pile standing up. For a coarse pile a wooden dowel-rod and a razor-blade can be used (with great care). Brass rods or smooth steel rods can be pulled out without cutting, and this leaves an uncut pile.

Designs can be made by cutting parts of the pile loops and leaving others. A commercial fabric of this type is moquette, cut and/or uncut.

170 Velvet, cross-section

(iv) *b* *Weft pile.* The corduroys are weft pile fabrics and are woven by a completely different system.

(*171a, b*) The back is again a firm plain or twill cloth, but the pile is a weft which floats across the cloth and is then tied into it by working through it round an odd number of ends (*a*). The floats are cut in the centre when the cloth is off the loom, and the pile stands up, round topped or square according to the length and weave of the floats (*b*). Typical cords are given in (*172*).

171 Corduroy, cross-section

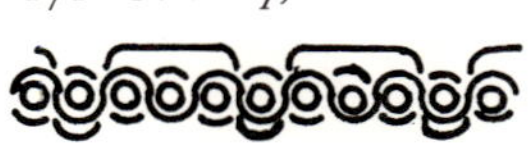

(a) Uncut

(b) Cut

				0	7 3 1	0					11 9 3 1
	0	0			10 4	0		0			13 75
0			0	0	9 5		0		0	0	14 8 2
	0				8 6 2				0		12 10 64
6	4	2 5	3	1		6	4	2 5	3	1	

172 Corduroy
(a) Drafts (redrawn from John Murphy's Treatise*)*

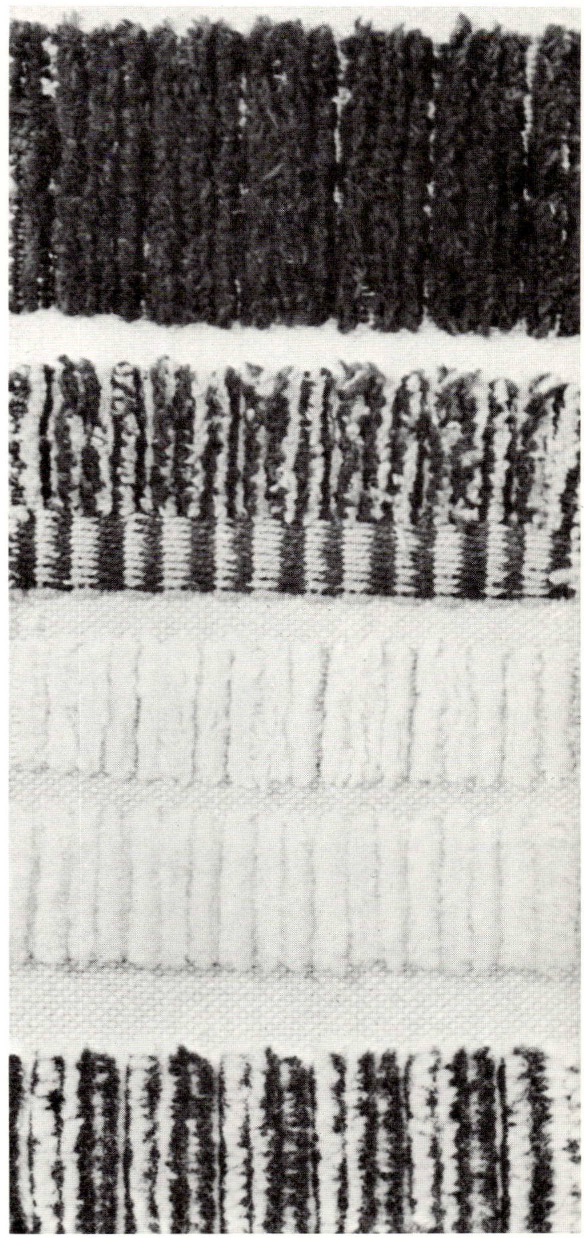

(b) Sampler

7 Double-faced weaves

A One warp and one weft

As there are two distinct sets of threads in a simple cloth, by bringing the majority of one set of threads to one face or the other a cloth with a different effect each side is produced. In a self-coloured cloth the difference is due to the varying reflection of light from the two sets of threads. With warp and weft of different colours the cloth will have one colour on each face. By bringing areas of warp face and weft face to the top of the cloth, stripe, check and figure designs are produced.

(i) Twills

(i) *a* *Weft-way stripes* Any unbalanced weave can be used, and is woven warp face and weft face for the two stripes. A three-shaft $\frac{2}{1}$ twill gives only a slight change of colour (*173*), and an eight-shaft $\frac{7}{1}$ twill a considerable change (*174*).

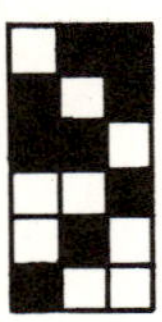

173 Three-end twills, warp face and weft face $\frac{2}{1}, \frac{1}{2}$

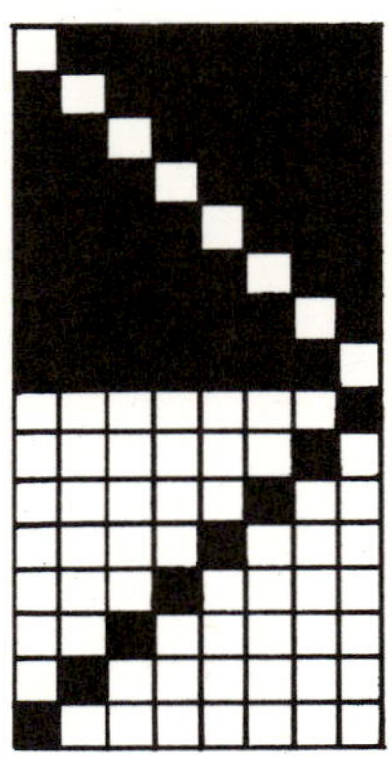

174 Eight-end twills, warp face and weft face $\frac{7}{1}, \frac{1}{7}$

It is better to reverse the weave when changing faces to prevent long floats occurring which will break the edges of the stripes.

A useful weave is the four-shaft broken twill (*175*), which gives an even texture without a solid twill line. The weave requires no more shafts, but twice as many treadles for the striped cloth as the plain cloth, or if this is not possible, a modified tie-up which will give the weave by using both feet for some of the sheds (see *The Technique of Weaving*, Introduction, and diagram 139, page 80).

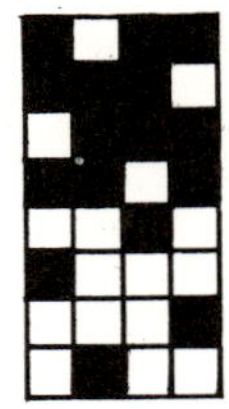

175 Four-end broken twill, warp and weft face

(i) *b* *Warp-way stripes* These are similar to weft-way stripes but require only the same number of treadles as the basic twill, but twice as many shafts. The stripes are drawn alternately on the front and back halves of the harness, and are tied so that the warp-faced and weft-faced weaves twill in opposite directions (*176*).

(i) *c* *Checks or two-block weaves* (*177a, b*) By combining weave (*a*) and weave (*b*) into one weave, i.e. reversing both threading and lifting, the warp and weft faces alternate to give checks. Twice as many shafts and treadles are needed.

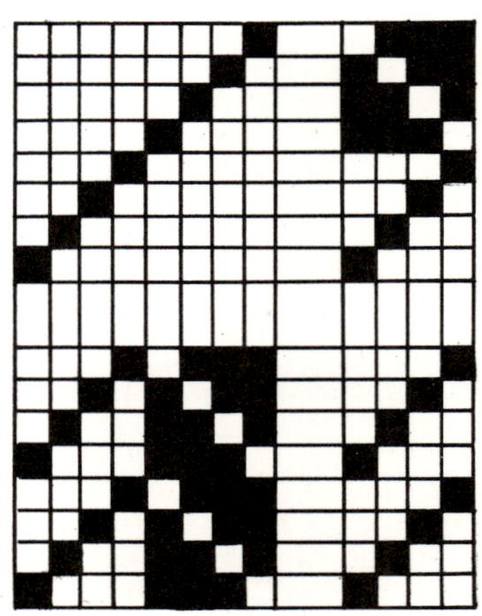

176 $\frac{1}{3}$ *and* $\frac{3}{1}$ *warp-way stripe*

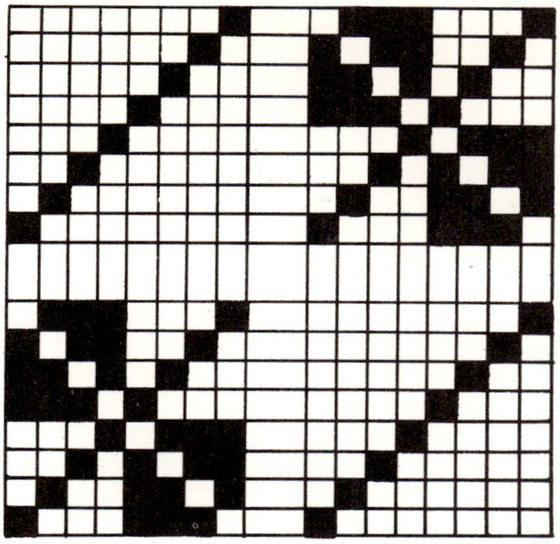

177 $\frac{3}{1}$ and $\frac{1}{3}$ check
(a) Weave diagram

177 *(b) Cloth*

(ii) Damask weaves

Originally a damask was a figured cloth with a design in weft satin on a warp satin, warp twill or fine rib ground. A type of all-over damask spot weave was called 'double damask' in the late eighteenth century, and a check or two-block pattern based on warp and weft satins or twills was called a 'diaper'. Nowadays damask and double damask are used indiscriminately for any type of patterned cloth using warp- and weft-faced satins for the design.

The simplest damask uses a two-block five-end satin weave, on ten shafts (*178*). If a counter-march loom is not available a special form of counter-balanced harness is used (see *The Technique of Weaving*, page 24, diagram 37). The satin weave, when used in this way, starts on the *second* end or pick so that the join at the corners of four adjacent squares has reasonably long floats. If the weave started on the first end a small rib of plain weave would be formed, and this would make a pinhole at every corner, and distort all the first and last ends and picks of each block (*179*).

178 *Two-block five-end damask, starting on second end*

179 *Two-block five end damask, starting incorrectly on first end*

Damasks may be woven on three, four or five blocks (and on a draw loom), but as each block needs five shafts and treadles a three-block design using fifteen shafts and treadles is the practical limit, though a four-block damask using a broken twill instead of a satin, and on sixteen shafts and treadles used to be quite common. Five-, six- and seven-block damasks can be woven in two other ways, either by using a special mounting on the loom, or by using a compound harness on an ordinary counter-march loom. The special mounting, using five treadles and a knob for each block is described by John Murphy in his *Treatise on the Art of Weaving*. The compound harness needs two harnesses, one of five shafts with long-eyed heddles for the ground, and one of standard heddles with as many shafts as there are blocks.

(*180*) shows a side view of the compound mounting, and (*181*) the threading draft and lifting plan of a two-block design in a five-end satin. The heddles of the figure harness have the five ends for one repeat of the weave drawn together in each eye, and these ends are separated when they are drawn in the ground harness (straight draft). The eyes of the ground harness are about 5 inches long, so that the figure harness can shed without being checked by the ground. The figure harness raises all the ends in the warp-faced blocks and sinks all the ends in the weft-faced blocks, so that the design is made without any weave, i.e. if a pick were thrown through the figure shed it would float loosely under or over the blocks. The ground harness raises one end and sinks another of each group of five ends, and leaves the other three in the centre of the shed. When the two harnesses are combined the figure harness divides all the ends, and the ground harness then raises one end in five on the weft-faced blocks, and vice versa on the warp-faced blocks. Thus the ground harness overrides the figure harness to construct the weave, and the figure harness raises or lowers the ends left in the shed by the ground harness (*180*). The figure treadles are operated by one foot, and held down for as many picks as required, whilst the other foot works heel and toe over the ground treadles.

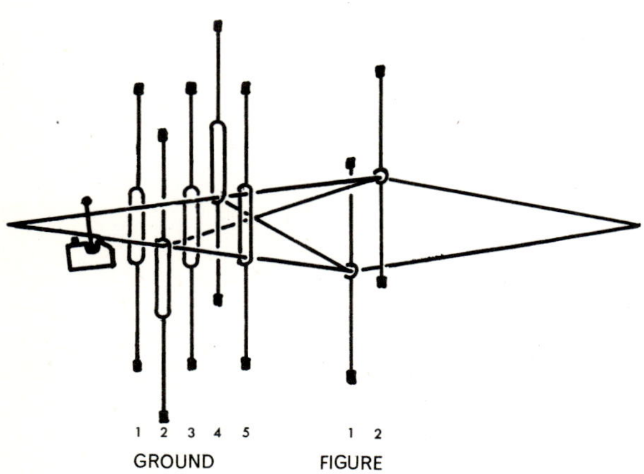

180 Compound mounting for two-block five-end damask (side view)

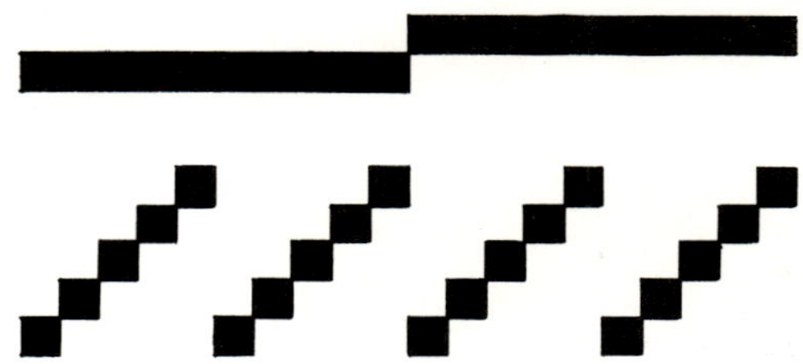

181 (a) Threading draft for 180

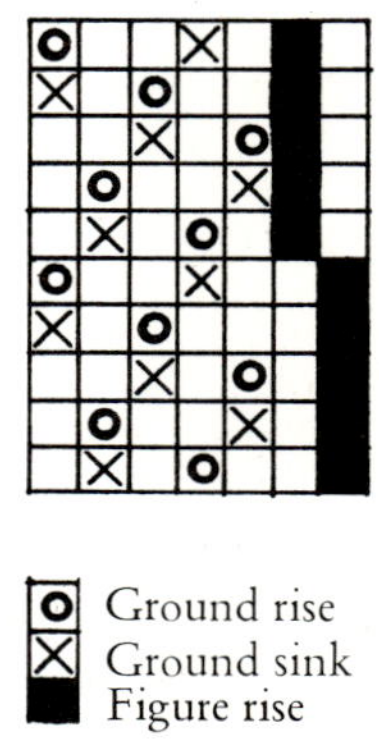

181 (b) Lifting for 180

(iii) Corkscrew weaves

These weaves are twilled ribs, warp or weft, but as one set of threads appears almost entirely on both faces they can be considered as double-faced weaves. The warp corkscrew is frequently used for scarves with longitudinal stripes, and this is the most popular use of it for hand-weavers.

The weave is based on a satin with an odd number of ends, and the smallest practicable number is seven.

(iii) *a Warp corkscrew* (*182a, b*) The satin weave is drafted with a move of two outwards (*a*), and then each stitching point is extended vertically to become a warp float of just *over* half the length of the repeat of the weave, four picks out of seven (*b*). The threading is straight draft on seven shafts, and the lifting plan is the same as the weave plan.

182 *Warp corkscrew developed warp way from seven end satin*

(a) Satin base

(b) Corkscrew, lifting as weave plan

With a fairly high sett the warp floats cover the weft, except for the single spot of weft in the satin weave on the back, which is usually negligible.

On eight shafts the weave cannot be a satin, as a move of two does not give a weave, so two rows of marks four picks apart are taken as the base, and the warp works $\frac{5}{3}$ (*183*).

183 *Warp corkscrew, eight ends*

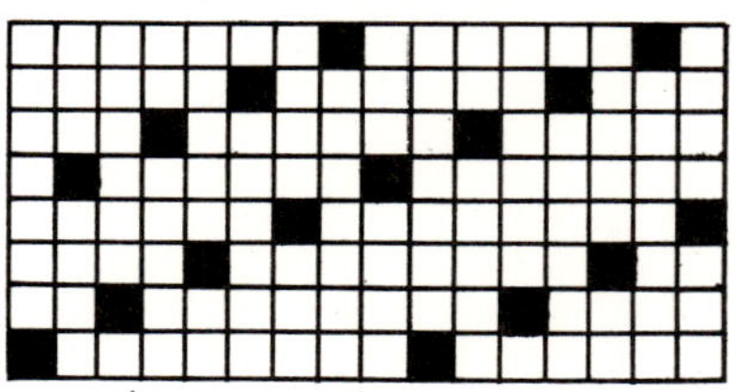

(a) Base

(b) Corkscrew weave, lifting as weave plan

(iii) *b Weft corkscrew* (*184a, b*) The seven-end satin is drafted with a move of two upwards (*a*), and the stitching point extended horizontally to become a warp float of just *under* half the length of the weave (*b*). This makes the weft predominate instead of the warp when using a normal sett and a firmer beat. The threading is straight, and the lifting plan is the same as the weave plan.

184 *Weft corkscrew developed weft way from seven-end satin*

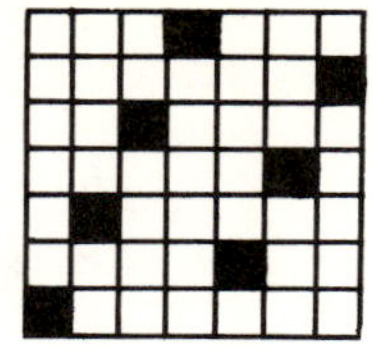

(a) Satin base

(b) Corkscrew, lifting as weave plan

B Backed weaves

(i) Weft-backed (double weft-faced) cloth

This type of cloth has a weft face on both sides, the stitching points of one face being covered by the weft floats of the other (*185*). The backing weave may, or may not, be the same as the face weave; a $\frac{1}{3}$ twill may be backed by a $\frac{3}{1}$ twill, a $\frac{2}{2}$ twill, or by a $\frac{2}{2}$ hopsack (*186a–c*).
The threading is four-shaft straight draft, and in the weave plan face and back picks are placed on alternate rows.

185 *Double weft-faced cloth, cross-section*

186 *Weft-backed $\frac{1}{3}$ twill*

(a) $\frac{1}{3}$ twill backed with $\frac{3}{1}$ twill
(b) $\frac{1}{3}$ twill backed with $\frac{2}{2}$ twill
(c) $\frac{1}{3}$ twill backed with a $\frac{2}{2}$ hopsack

(*187a–d*) A warp end should never go directly from front to back of the cloth as this causes distortion and pinholes. (*a*) shows a section through the weft with one end interlacing with four picks of the face, (*b*) an end working through four back picks, (*c*) both (*a* and *b*) combined correctly, with the end going between the two faces as it passes from surface to surface, and (*d*) the same, but incorrectly stitched, with pinholes occurring at the arrows. Although a cloth of equal faces has been used as an example, a weft-backed cloth often has a fine warp and face weft, and a coarse back weft, working two face picks to one back pick to give a fine surface but a heavy cloth.

187 Weft-backed fabric, cross-sections

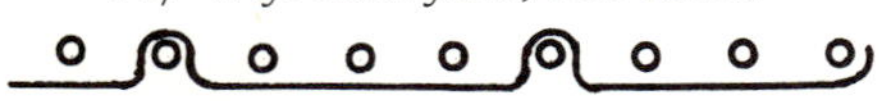

(a) Face weft

(b) Backing weft

(c) Warp end showing correct stitching

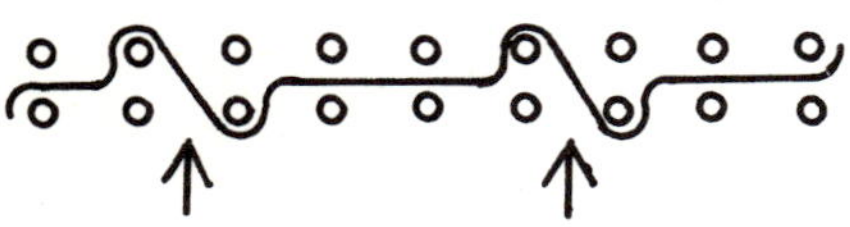

(d) Warp end showing incorrect stitching

188 Two-block weft-backed fabric

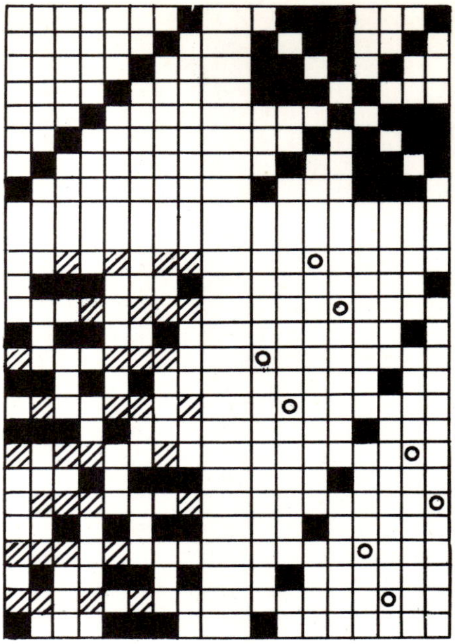

(a) Weave diagram

(ii) Warp-backed (double warp-faced) cloth

This is very similar to the weft-backed cloth, and the whole of the previous section applies if warp is substituted for weft and vice versa, and the diagrams turned through 90 degrees. It will require eight shafts and four treadles for the example given, instead of four shafts and eight treadles, and a two-coloured warp (end and end) and one shuttle, instead of a self-coloured warp and two shuttles for a plain-coloured cloth (*188*).

There is, of course, no reason why both cloths should not have colour and weave effects, or simple stripes or overchecks on the two faces, provided that the spots of colour on both faces due to the common set of threads can be incorporated satisfactorily into the patterns.

(iii) Two-block backed weaves

Although both warp and weft backing are possible the warp-backed two-block cloth needs sixteen shafts, so is somewhat impracticable.

The weft-backed cloth is threaded and tied up as for a two-block double-faced weave with a single warp and weft (*177*), and woven as a plain weft-backed fabric. The two wefts will pass from front to back of the cloth at the edges of the stripes, and checks are woven by breaking the sequence of the colouring. Treadles from each half of the tie-up are used alternately. In (*188*) the same tie-up is used as in *177* to show the similarity between them, though neither would be used in practice without rearranging them to work heel and toe over the treadles (see Introduction).
Cloths with two face picks to one back pick, etc can be woven.

188 (b) Cloth

8 Double weave

(i) Plain cloth

Two plain cloths, one above the other, can be woven on a four-shaft straight draft if they are completely separate or joined only at the edges.

(*189*) By lifting shafts 1 and 3 alternately the face cloth is woven, and by holding 1 and 3 up and lifting 2 and 4 with them alternately the back is woven. With two shuttles the fabrics are separate.

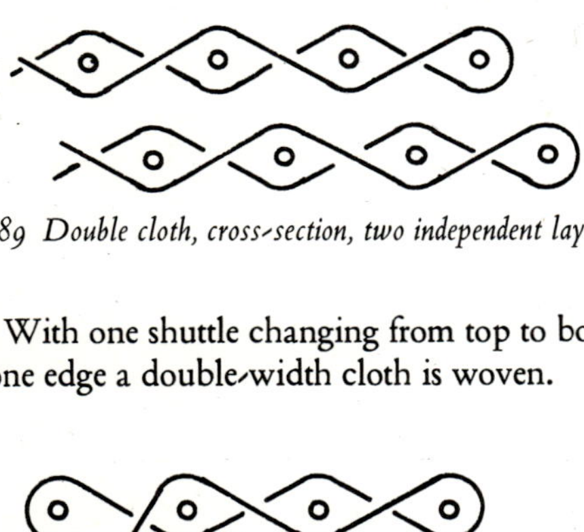

189 Double cloth, cross-section, two independent layers

(*190*) With one shuttle changing from top to bottom at only one edge a double-width cloth is woven.

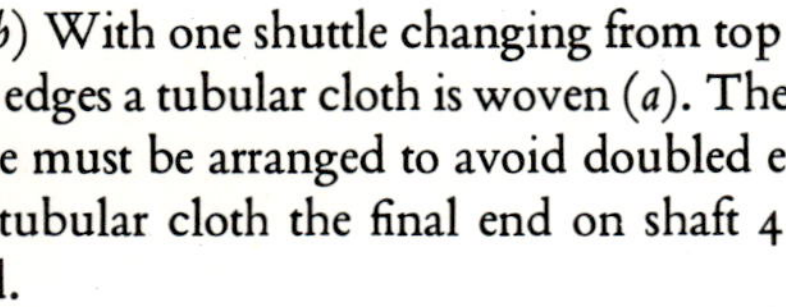

190 Double cloth, cross-section, double width

(*191a, b*) With one shuttle changing from top to bottom at both edges a tubular cloth is woven (*a*). The change at the edge must be arranged to avoid doubled ends (*b*). In the tubular cloth the final end on shaft 4 has to be omitted.

191 Double cloth, cross-section, tubular cloth

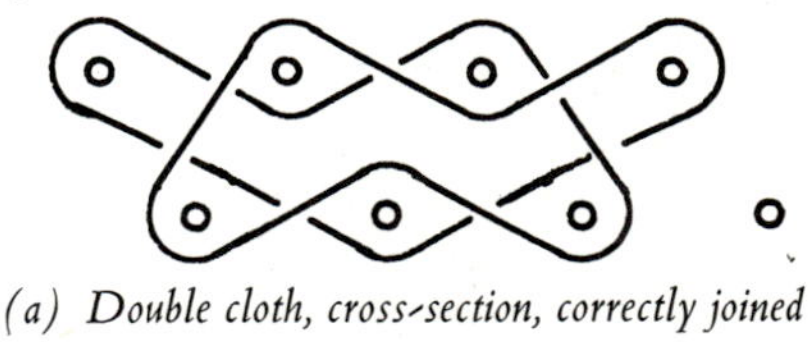

(a) Double cloth, cross-section, correctly joined

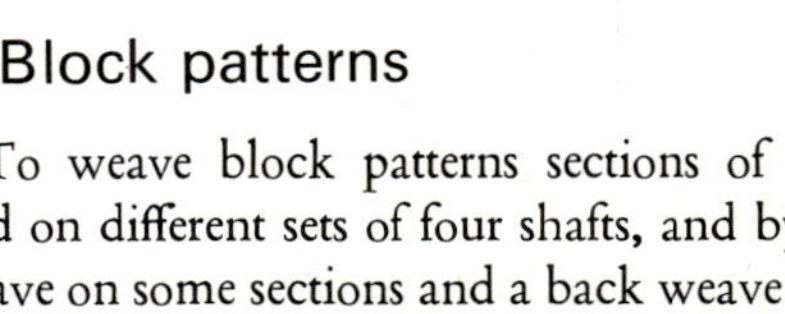

(b) Double cloth, cross-section, incorrectly joined

(ii) Block patterns

(*192*) To weave block patterns sections of warp are threaded on different sets of four shafts, and by lifting a face weave on some sections and a back weave on others for the same shed, the weft can be made to pass from front to back of the cloth a number of times in the width of the cloth.

Regarded in another way, the face ends are opened for the width of the cloth, and the back ends are alternately in the top or bottom of the shed. If a face weave and back weave are used in succession on the same section the warp does the same, i.e. passes from front to back at the change of weave. The cloth will then consist of small square pockets of double cloth joined at the edges where the threads change faces.

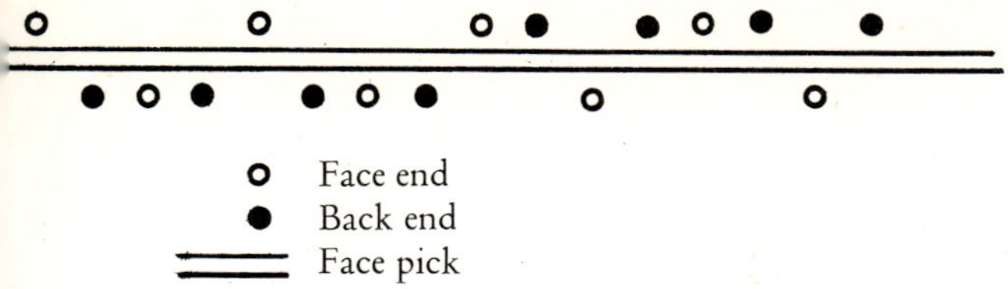

192 Double plain cloth, two-block, cross-section through one shed

(*193a*) is a cross-section of such a cloth, and the same warp way and weft way. Each individually controlled block will need four shafts, so three- and four-block patterns will require twelve and sixteen shafts respectively. To reduce the number of shafts a compound mounting is used, with a ground harness of four shafts, and a figure harness with two shafts for each block. The figure harness at the back has the usual small-eyed heddles, and the ground harness in front has long-eyed heddles ($4\frac{1}{2}$ inches). The warp is entered face and back alternately. The back pair of shafts of the figure harness carries the face and back ends respectively for the width of the first block, and the next pair the ends of the second block, and so on. The warp is next drawn through the long-eyed ground harness in a straight threading (face, back, face, back), so that each end is drawn once in each harness. (*193b*) is a double woven cloth (see page 82).

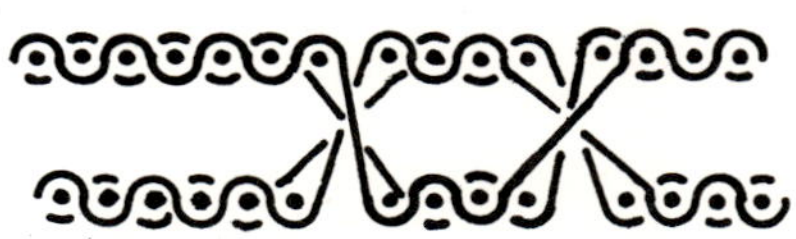

193 (a) Double plain cloth, two-block, cross-section

(*194*) is the threading draft for a two-block pattern. When the back (fourth) shaft of the figure harness is raised it lifts all the face ends of the odd blocks, and the third lifts all the back ends of the same blocks, the second and first lifting face and back ends of the even blocks. The figure harness can work without being affected by the ground harness because of the long eyes of the latter.

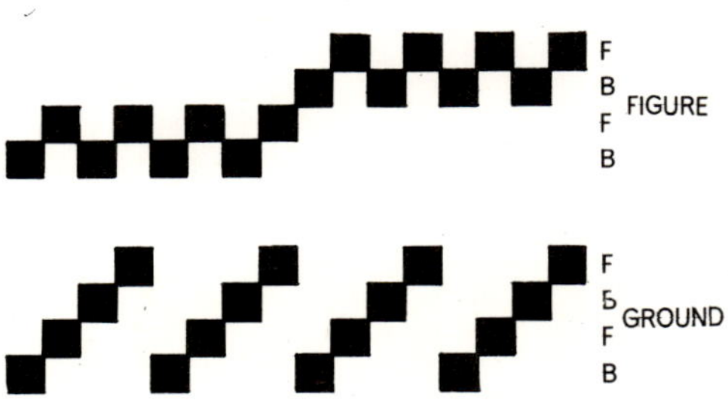

194 Threading draft for compound mounting for (193)

(*195*) When a face pick is being woven (ground shaft 4) to show on the even blocks, the back ends of the odd blocks can be raised above it with shaft 3 of the figure harness, and the back ends of the even blocks held down below it with shaft 1.

On the back pick which follows (ground shaft 3) the face ends of the even blocks are held up with shaft 2, and those of the odd blocks held down with shaft 4. The ends remaining in the centre of the figure shed will be divided by the ground harness, and ends divided by the figure harness are unaffected by the ground shafts through which they are drawn as those will then remain stationary.

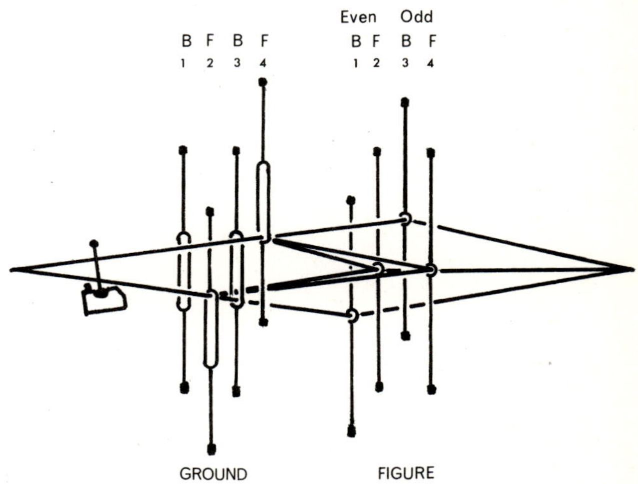

195 Compound mounting for (193), side view

(*196*) is the lifting plan for the same weave.

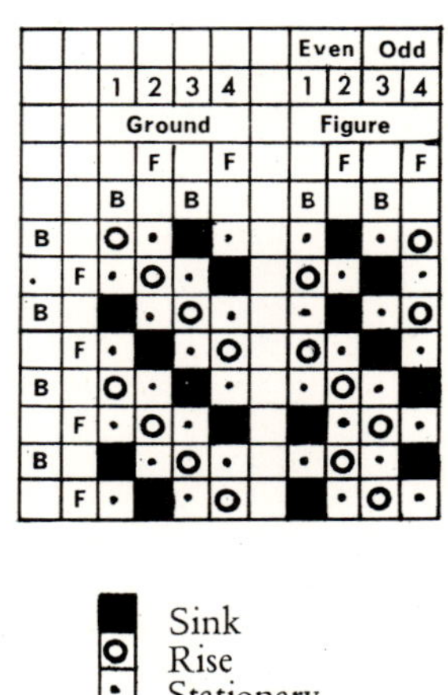

196 Lifting plan for (194)

193 (b) Four block double woven cloth (old Welsh bed cover)

9 Gauze and leno weaves

These weaves come into the category of cross-weaving, in which a thread or threads partially twist round another thread or threads. The basic cloth is called 'gauze', and if the gauze weave is combined with any other the fabric is called 'leno'.

In the basic gauze one end crosses one other, the end which is held firmly is called the 'standard' (or 'standing') end, and the other the 'crossing' end. Four shafts are needed, and usually an easer bar to take the tension off the crossing end on the crossed shed.

(*197*) gives the threading and lifting of two types of gauze. Shaft 1 is called the 'doup', shaft 2 the 'front crossing' shaft, shaft 3 the 'standard' (shaft), and shaft 4 the 'back crossing' shaft.

The left side of the diagram shows left- and right-hand crossing, and the right side shows all right-hand crossing. The standard end, shown white in the diagram and the photographs is drawn in shaft 3 (standard) only. The crossing end (black) is drawn in shaft 4 (back crossing shaft), crossed under its standard end, and then drawn in shaft 1 (doup), which is not a full heddle, but a half heddle or doup attached in this case to the lower shaft stick of the front shaft. The free end of the doup is threaded through the eye (or the eye and upper doup) of the heddle on the second shaft (front crossing shaft).

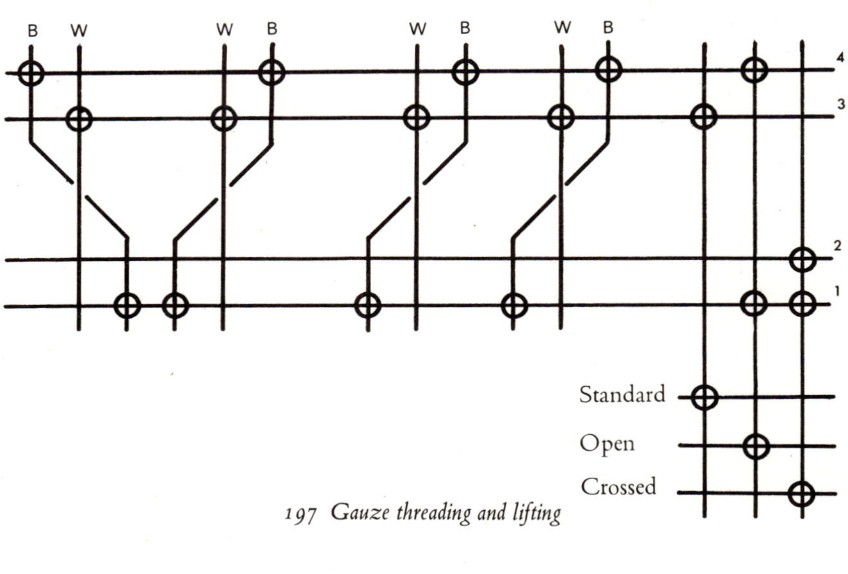

197 Gauze threading and lifting

(*198a, b*) shows a string doup in a wire heald such as could be made up for a table loom (*a*), and a string doup in a string heddle for a foot power loom (*b*).
A doup can be hung from the top, and the crossing end brought above the standard end, but the bottom doup is usually preferred as it drops out of the way when it breaks, and does not tangle with the warp.

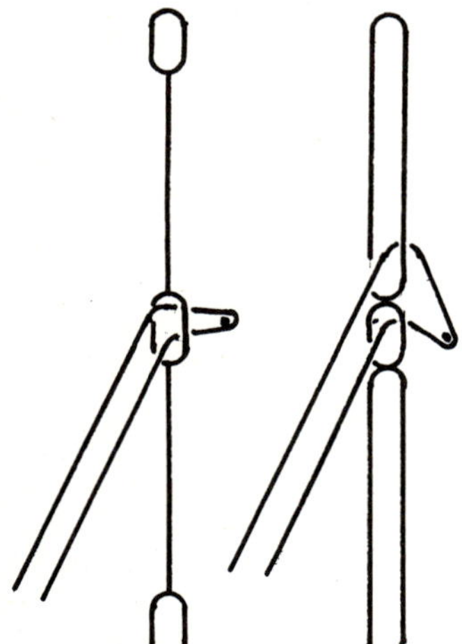

(a) *(b)*

198 Doups

There are three sheds, standard, open, and crossed. (*199a–d*) shows the initial position of the standard and crossing ends. The standard (or plain) shed is formed by raising the standard, shaft 3, (*b*) and (*200*). The open shed, with the crossing end on its normal or open side of the standard end is formed by raising the back crossing shaft, 4, and at the same time raising the doup, shaft 1, to allow it to run freely through the eye of the front crossing shaft 2, (*c*) and (*201*). The crossed shed is formed by raising the doup, shaft 1, and the front crossing shaft, 2, together, so that the doup pulls the crossing end under the standard end and up on the crossed side, (*d*) and (*202*).

The crossing ends must work in the same dent of the reed to allow the crossing to take place, and though this is straight forward on simpler fabrics, special reeds (see chapter 12) are necessary for weaves in which one end crosses a group of ends, unless loose doups (see chapter 12) tied to a spare shaft are used in front of the reed.

When the standard and open sheds are used alternately the fabric is a simple plain weave. Alternating the standard and crossed sheds still gives plain weave, but in the crossed position (see below). The open and crossed sheds, with the standard end held down gives the gauze weave.

199 Gauze sheds

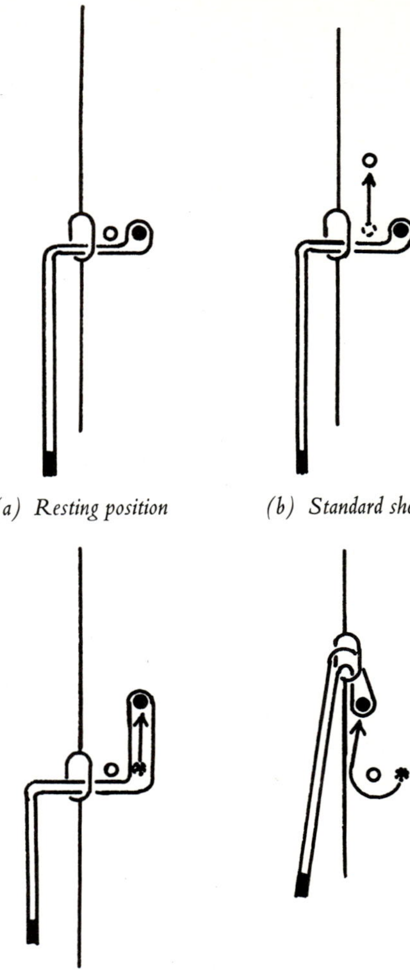

(a) Resting position *(b) Standard shed*

(c) Open shed *(d) Crossed shed*

200 Gauze standard shed, S

201 Gauze open shed, O

202 Gauze crossed shed, X

(*203*) If these two sheds (open and crossed) alternate throughout the cloth is pure gauze.

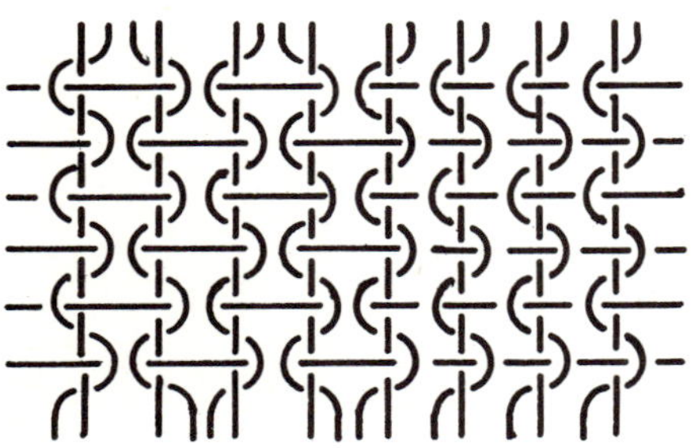

203 Gauze cloth weave plan

(*204*) If a crossed shed is followed by several plain sheds on either open or crossed sides the weave is leno. Cellular (not honeycomb) blankets and lightly woven cellular clothing are leno weaves, plain net curtains are usually gauze weave.

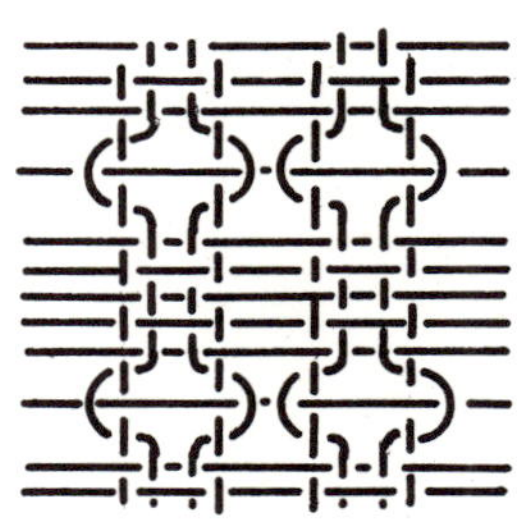

204 Leno cloth weave plan

(*205a, b*) Another leno weave forms a series of small holes in rows across the fabric, rather like hemstitching, by working the crossing end on the open side for one stripe, and on the crossed side for the next stripe.
(*a*) shows all right-hand crossing, (*b*) right- and left-hand crossing.

The plain gauze is useful for stoles, light scarves, and as a ground for light panels and hangings. Though either form can be used, crossing left and right is generally more even than crossing one way, as the latter often developes unpleasant slopes in the weft.

205 *Leno cloth weave plan*

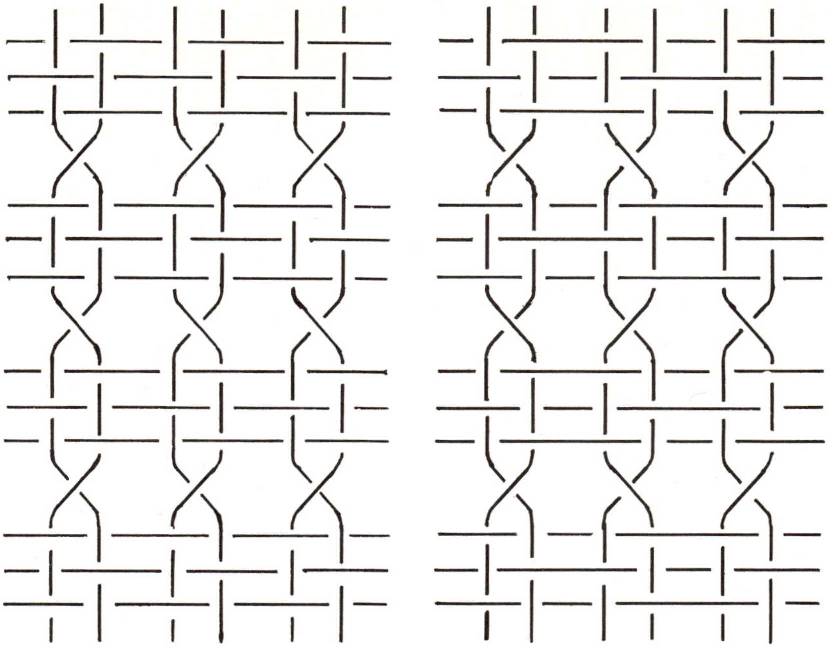

(*a*) *Crossing ends all left to right* (*b*) *Crossing ends alternately to left and right*

(*206*) The cellular leno weave, which is the weave imitated by the mock leno, needs to cross left and right to throw the weft into a series of level floats in two layers. The five plain picks run together, and form small pockets in the cloth, and the single crossed pick (often a doubled pick caught by the selvedge), twists the ends in the opposite way to the pick on either side, and is itself thrown up to the surface of the cloth on both sides.

206 *Cross-section of leno cloth*

(*207*) Examples of gauze and leno fabrics.

Owing to the various tensions in the cloth on the loom it loses a good 25 per cent in width and length when relaxed in the finishing. The selvedge should be woven plain or hopsack, the latter needing two extra shafts and the former one extra, the selvedge ends being drawn alternately on the back crossing shaft and the extra shaft. The other leno referred to would have a similar selvedge on the standard and one extra shaft.

Stripes of other weaves can be placed between stripes, or even pairs of ends, of leno weave. The extra warp is threaded on shafts placed in the existing space between the front pair and back pair of shafts of the gauze harness. These shafts virtually form a separate harness which works independently of the gauze, and a second warp beam is needed for that part of the warp. A second beam is not necessary for plain gauze and leno if the standard and crossing ends are to be equally bent in the cloth, though an easer bar will still be needed. This may be nothing more than a dowel-rod and weights (see chapter 12).

The back crossing shaft and the standard are frequently mounted the other way round, with the standard at the back of the harness. Each way has its own advantages, for different types of weaving, but in either case, the space between the front pair of shafts and the back pair is more important. It should be as large as is practicable to lessen the strain on the crossing ends on the crossed shed.

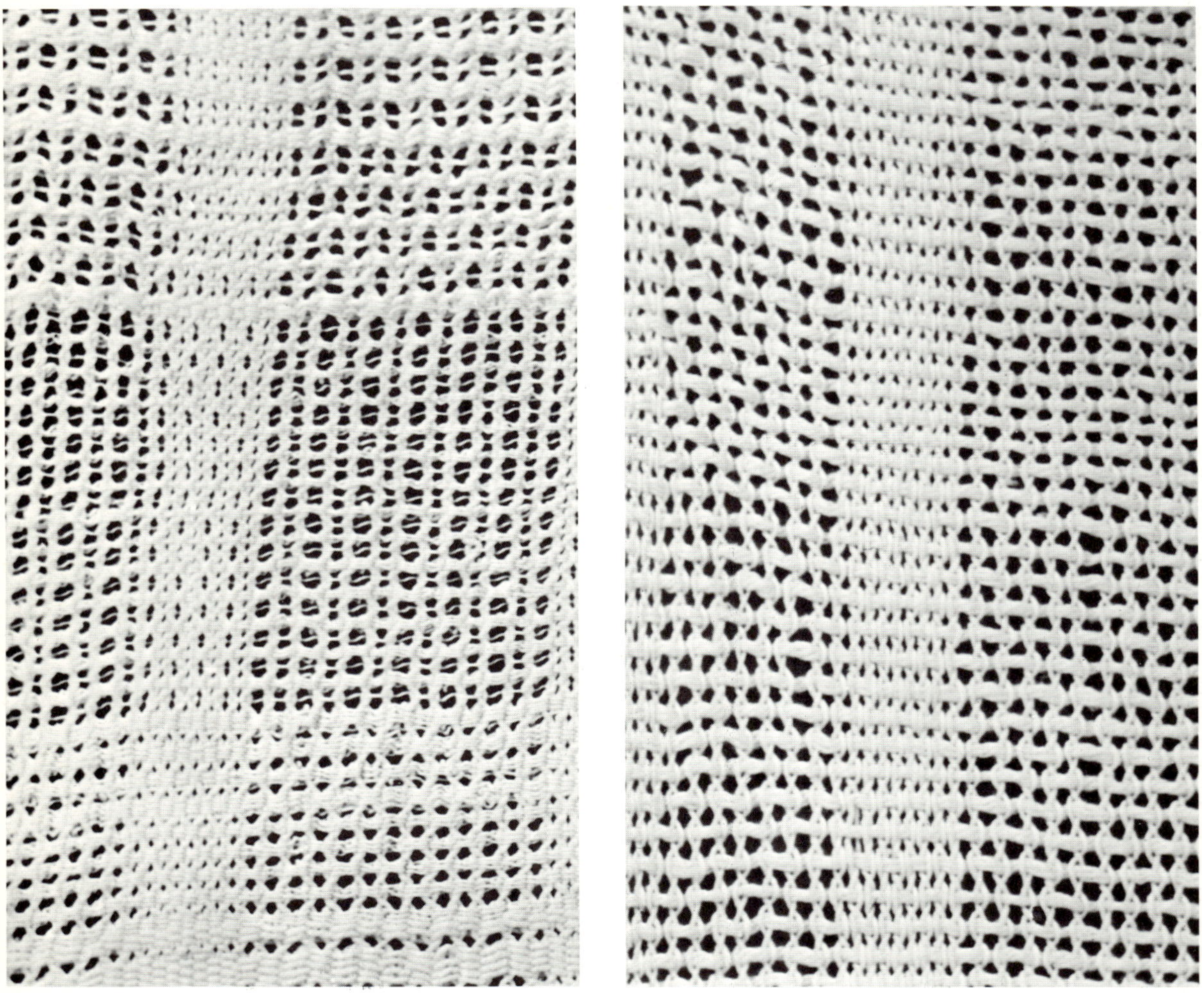

207 Gauze and leno cloth

10 Colour and weave effects

These designs are used for fabrics in which each thread is visible, as they depend on the colours of the individual threads and their exact relationship to the weave. They differ from simple stripe and check designs in that the warp and weft colours are broken by the weave, and the appearance of the weave is obscured by the colours which show on the surface of the cloth regardless of whether they are warp or weft.

The weaves can best be grouped by the general effect, i.e. simple or all-over, warp stripe, weft stripe and check. The simplest designs are small, and the warp and weft are often of different colouring plans. The stripe designs and check designs arise from the interaction between three factors. The warp and weft orders of colouring can both be simple or compound, and the weave can be simple warp stripe, weft stripe or check. The last three are not of great interest to the handweaver as they usually require a minimum of eight shafts to be interesting, and often twelve or sixteen.

(*208*) The designs can be worked out quite easily on point paper. First the weave plan is filled in lightly in pencil, and the order of colouring for warp and weft indicated along the top and down the side. The ends are taken one at a time and followed down the weave. If the marks on the weave plan indicate warp up, the colour is filled in on the marked squares, and the unmarked (weft) squares left blank. If only two colours are being used the darker one is marked and the lighter ends left untouched. Next the picks are taken in a similar way, except that the blanks on the weave plan are now filled in with the correct colour as they indicate weft up. By looking at the point-paper design through a magnifying glass (counting glass or linen prover) held at some distance from the eye a fairly good idea of the effect in the cloth is obtained.

(i) Simple all-over effects

These are obtained on a simple weave with simple orders of warping and wefting, which need not necessarily be the same. They can be Bird's Eye (small spot pattern), line, hair line, stepped line, or Dog's Tooth (or Shepherd's Check). The table gives a few of the more common effects.

208 Colour and weave, showing light and dark thread marked on the upper and left edges; top left weave plan marked; top right dark ends marked; bottom left dark picks marked; bottom right final weave plan

Weave	*Warping order*	*Wefting order*	*Effect*
Plain	1 1	1 1	Line
	1 2	2 1	Interlocking I s
	1 1	2 2	Serrated line
	2 2	2 2	Bird's Eye
	2 3	2 3	Spots
Hopsack	1 1	1 1	Stepped line
	1 1	2 2	Line
	1 1	4 4	Line
	2 2	2 2	*Bird's Eye
	2 2	4 4	*Line
	4 4	4 4	*Bird's Eye
Twill	1 1	2 2	Serrated line
$\frac{3}{1}$ or $\frac{1}{3}$	2 2	2 2	Dog's Tooth
	2 2	4 4	*Serrated line
	4 4	4 4	Bird's Eye
Twill	Self-colour	2 2	Spots
$\frac{2}{2}$	1 1	1 1	Stepped line
	1 1	2 2	Bird's Eye
	1 1	4 4	*Line
	2 2	2 2	Line
	2 2	4 4	*Serrated line
	4 4	4 4	*Dog's Tooth

NOTE (*a*)* different effects on different footings.
(*b*) warp and weft can be interchanged when their colouring orders are different.

In some of the combinations listed above the design can be changed from warp way to weft way by interchanging the order of warping and wefting. In many of the hopsacks and twills the design can be altered considerably by putting the colouring on a different footing in relation to the weave. This can be done by starting the weave one or more picks later in the case of twills, or combining different pairs of shafts in the hopsacks (e.g. shafts 2 and 3, 4 and 1 instead of 1 and 2, 3 and 4). The weft can be altered simply by starting the colouring plan on a different pick of the weave.

(ii) Warp stripe

When the relative positions of the colouring plan and weave are altered, a different effect is produced, and warp (and weft) stripes are woven by exploiting this change of effect.

(*209*) The simpler method is to use a simple warping and simple weave and alter the footing of the colour by doubling the number of ends in a unit of colour at intervals.

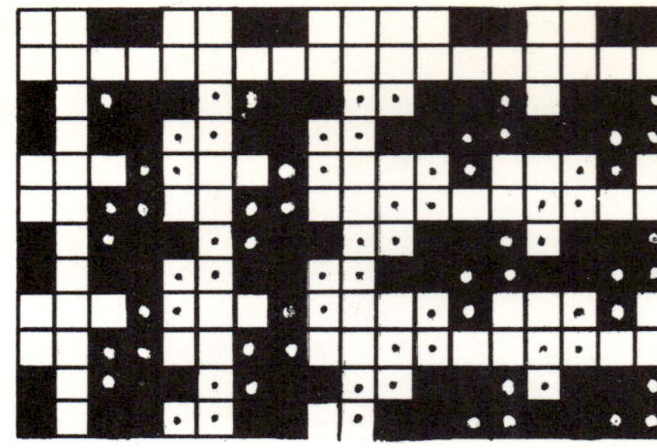

209 Change of colouring, $\frac{2}{2}$ twill with 2 and 2 colouring

(*210*) The same effect is obtained by putting the weave on a different footing by cutting and reversing like a herringbone.

A simple weave can be used with a compound warp, i.e. 2 and 2 stripe alternating with a 4 and 4 stripe or a 1 and 1 stripe. The opposite is also true, a compound weave and simple warping will give a warp stripe, but more shafts are usually needed, except for 2 and 2 twill combined with 2 and 2 hopsack or weft rib.

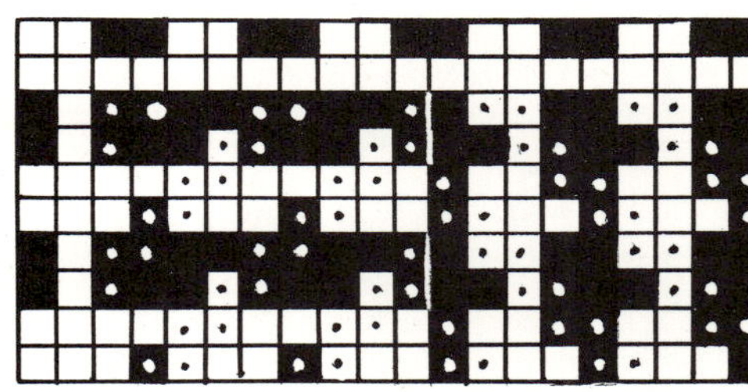

210 Change of weave, $\frac{2}{2}$ herringbone twill with 2 and 2 colouring, with weave starting one pick later than (209)

(iii) Weft stripe

Weft stripes are formed in a similar way by breaking the order of wefting or of lifting. The broken weft colouring is the easier way, as often a four-shaft weave sufficiently different to have any great effect will have a different take-up and cause uneven selvedges. With more complex weaves on eight or more shafts it is easier to plan obviously dissimilar weaves which still have approximately equal take-ups.

(iv) Checks

(*211a–c*) A combination of warp and weft stripes will give a check, and again the easiest way is to break both orders of colouring to save altering the threading and lifting. The well-known basket weave pattern is an excellent example.

211 Basket weave in $^{2}_{2}$ hopsack (2 and 2 colouring)

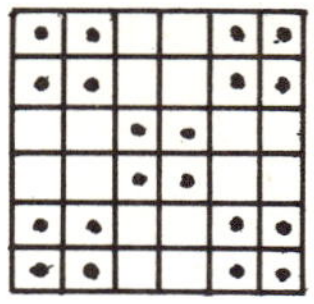

(a) Weave plan

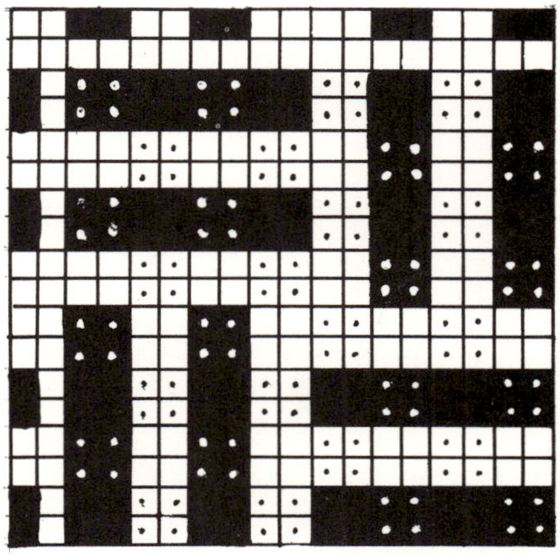

(b) Colouring plan broken to change direction of lines

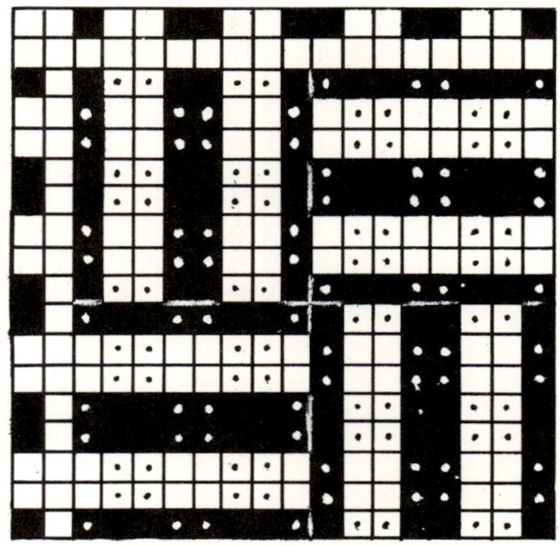

(c) Weave broken to change direction of lines

(*212*) Basket weave cloth in plain weave with 1 and 1 colouring.

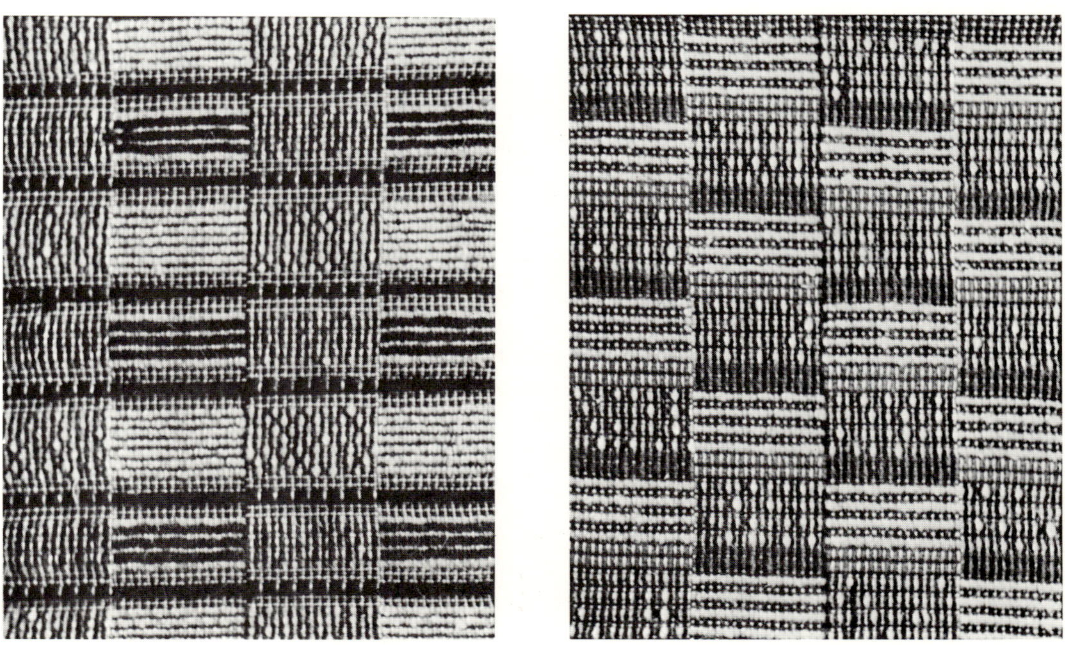

212 Basket weave cloth in plain weave with 1 and 1 colouring

11 Counts and setts for typical cloths

The firmness of a cloth is governed by three main factors, the count and the sett of the yarns, and the weave employed. These factors are interdependent, and if one is altered at least one other must be altered correspondingly to maintain a similar degree of firmness.

The weave in which the threads are most firmly supported by the intersections is the plain weave, which therefore needs fewer threads per inch than any other weave using identical yarns. As each pair of threads of one set is intersected by a thread of the other set, only half of the maximum number of threads per inch can be used in the cloth, and even then the cloth will be too firm for most purposes. Slightly more than three-quarters of this number is usually sufficient.

In twills and hopsacks two or more threads lie together in the cloth, so the sett has to be higher to compensate for the diminished support. Two-thirds of the maximum number of threads to the inch is the most that can be used in a $\frac{2}{2}$ twill or hopsack, and as in the plain weave, about three-quarters of this sett will produce a more useful cloth.

In satin weaves there is little support from the intersections, so a good rough guide is to put as many ends per inch in the warp as will just go into the inch when lying side by side without cramming together.

The same rule applies in the warp and weft rib weaves. The set of threads which form the ribs, and therefore do all the bending, should be as close as possible, while the straight threads of the other set obey the setting rule for the type of weave in which they work similarly, i.e. if the straight threads work singly they will set as a plain weave, if they work in pairs they will set as a $\frac{2}{2}$ hopsack, etc.

Cloths with a plain weave face, such as piqué, are set as for the plain weave itself. The stitching ends are extra to the plain weave, and as they intersect comparatively little with the face they do not need special consideration. A Bedford cord, however, needs a higher sett than a plain cloth as it needs to distort in the finishing, and can be set about half-way between a plain weave and a satin weave.

A mock leno can be set as firmly as a plain cloth, and the weave will open up in the finishing, especially if the ends are grouped in the reed. It can be set more lightly for special purposes.

Honeycombs need the threads fairly close together, and should be set about half-way between a plain weave and the maximum.

The traditional overshot weaves are set according to the way that they are to be woven. If they are woven in the usual way with a plain ground they are set as for a plain cloth. If they are woven with each pattern weft followed by its opposite, i.e. shafts 1 and 2 raised followed by shafts 3 and 4 raised without any plain ground then they can be set as for a weft rib weave.

The rule-of-thumb method for finding the maximum number of threads which will go into 1 inch is to wrap them round a ruler so that they touch without crowding, but a more accurate method is to calculate the yarn diameter (see *The Technique of Weaving*, page 78, paragraph 3). This, in both cases, gives the maximum number of threads per inch, from which the sett of the weave is calculated.

Cloths which are to be shrunk fairly heavily should be set correspondingly lighter and wider, i.e. a cloth to be shrunk by one-eighth of its width should be one-eighth more open and one-eighth wider on the loom.

The different yarn count systems now in use are gradually being replaced by the Tex system, based on metric units. Like the denier it is a direct system, and the count number is the weight in grammes of 1,000 metres of yarn.

Conversions

1 To convert from denier to tex or vice versa:
Denier divided by 9 equals tex.
Tex multiplied by 9 equals denier.

2 To convert from an indirect system to tex or vice versa:
Conversion factor divided by the indirect count equals tex.
Conversion factor divided by tex equals the indirect count.

Conversion factors

Woollen:	Galashiels	2480
	Yorkshire skein	1938
	West of England	1550
	Worsted	885·8
	Cotton	590·5
	Linen, wet spun	1654
	Spun silk	590·5
	American cut	1654
	American run	310

One advantage of tex is that all yarns of the same tex count will have the same sett in similar weaves, apart from slight allowances for hard and soft yarns (such as cotton and wool), and for looser or firmer fabrics.

In the table which follows the tex count is given in the first column, the usual count for yarns generally obtainable in the centre columns, with the resultant count (the thickness of the equivalent singles yarn) in the case of plied yarns (worsted and cotton), and the average sett for plain weave and $\frac{2}{2}$ twill in the last column. The slight discrepancies in the steady reduction of the ends per inch are due to the different settings needed for hard and soft yarns.

Tex count	Cotton		Woollen		Worsted		Linen wet spun & American cut	American run	Setts soft/hard yarns	
	Singles	Plied	Galashiels cut	Yorkshire woollen skein	Singles	Plied			Plain weave	Twill weave
49	12	2/24							36	48
55					16	2/32			32	42
59	10	2/20							32	42
63					14	2/28			30	40
65	9			30					30	40
69				28					28	36
74	8	3/24							28	36
78								4	25	34
81				24					25	34
84	7								25	34
88					10	2/20			25	34
97				20					22	30
98	6	3/18							24	32
103								3	22	30
118	5								22	30
124								2½	20	30
138				14			12		18/20	26/28
148	4								20	26
155			16					2	18	24
162				12					18	24
165							10		18/20	24/26
196	3	4/12							18	22
207			12				8	1½	16	20/22
226			11						15	20
276			9						14	18
277				7			6		14	18/20
292			8½						14	18
295	2	2/4							14	18
310			8					1	12	16
332							5		12	16/18
413							4		12	15
550			4½				3		8/10	12/14
590·5	1								10	14
620								½	9	12
827							2		8	10/12
885·8					1					
1654							1			
1938				1						
2480			1							

The setts are calculated from Ashenhurst's formula with a rather generous allowance of 20 to 25 per cent less than the full square sett, instead of the more usual 10 to 15 per cent, which tends to give cloths too closely set for hand-weaving.

The setts must necessarily be only a guide, particularly when using an unknown yarn, as hard and soft spinning or plying will affect the sett considerably. The column for linen and American cut is a good example of this variation the softer yarn setting approximately two ends per inch less than the harder one throughout the range shown.

12 Loom modifications

(i) Extra warp roller

Several weaves require a second warp roller, and this can be improvised quite easily, even for a foot power loom, from a piece of wood about 2 inches square and 1 foot longer than the loom is wide. The warp is looped over a warp lath which is tied on to the square beam and then wound on as usual. The improvised beam is lashed firmly across the back of the loom. When winding on during weaving the lashings are loosened, the beam turned to let off sufficient warp, and then re-tied. The second warp is slightly over-tightened with the cloth roller, and finally the warp beam on the loom tensioned to take off the slight over-tensioning on the second warp.

(ii) Gauze modifications

(ii) *a* *Easer bar* (*213a, b*) The crossing ends are taken under a dowel-rod, which is fastened down in the loom whilst tying on, to provide sufficient slack. The rod is weighted at each end, or springs tied between the rod and the bottom of the loom frame. A cord runs from the rod, over a pulley or pulleys, and down to the crossed shed treadle so that the dowel-rod rises on the crossed shed to ease the tension on the warp. When the treadle is released the weights fall and take up the slack in the crossing ends. The cross sticks have to be tied to the back of the loom to provide a fixed point over which the crossing ends can slide. On a table loom or a Danish-type foot power loom the cord from the dowel-rod runs straight to the pulley on the top castle, and a second cord is fastened between the back beam and the rod to prevent it pulling forward (dotted lines). If trouble is experienced in changing from the crossed to the open sheds the standard shed should be treadled between them to allow the weights to fall sufficiently.

213 *Gauze easer, improvised*

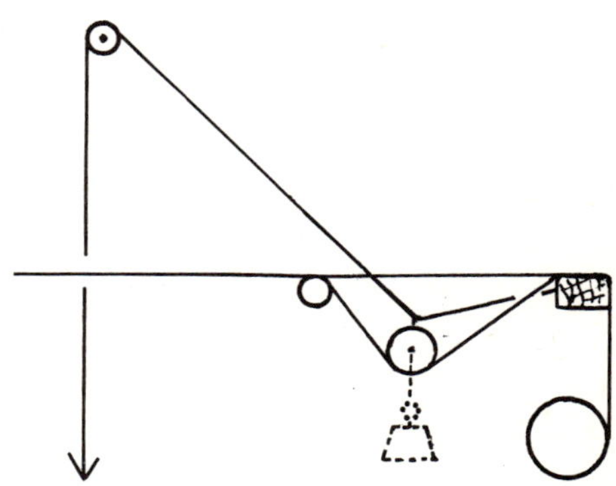

(a) Table loom or light (Danish-type) foot power loom

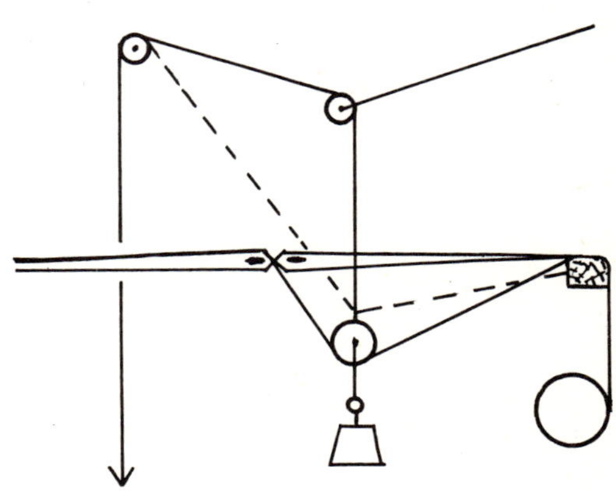

(b) Heavy foot power loom (English or Swedish type)

(ii) *b* *Loose doup* (*214a, b*) If a thick extra warp end is required to cross a group of ground ends, say one crossing four, a set of loose doups is used between the reed and the cloth. They are tied an inch or two longer than twice the depth of the shed, and are fastened to a spare shaft stick suspended from the top of the beater or from the top castle (*a*). Each doup encloses its own end, goes under the group of ends to be crossed, and is brought up through the warp and looped on the stick (*b*). The crossing end is normally down, floating on the underside of the cloth which is woven face down. It is brought up by its own ordinary shaft in the harness to stitch it in every few picks. When the spare shaft carrying the doup is raised the crossing end goes under the group of ground ends and is raised on the crossed side for that pick.

Doups can cross all the same way, or right and left hand as required.

214 Loose doup in front of reed

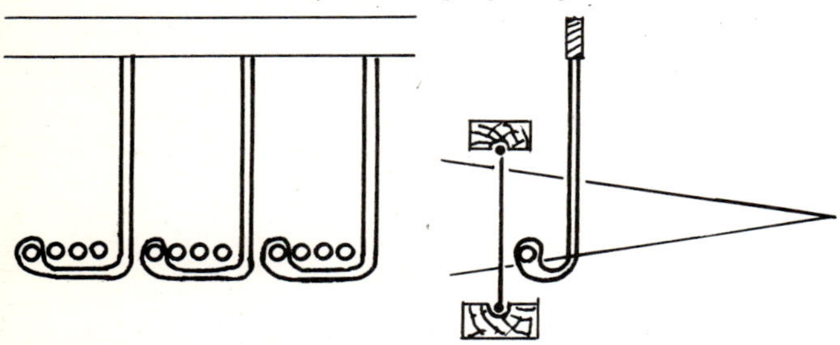

(a) Cross-section through warp (b) Diagrammatic cross-section along warp

(ii) *c* *Reeds* (*215*) If long lengths of this type of cloth are to be woven a normal gauze harness is used in conjunction with a special reed instead of a loose doup shaft. The gauze reed has a series of U-shaped wires and a vertical wire between repeats. The crossing end slides round the outermost U, and the ground ends are drawn in the others.

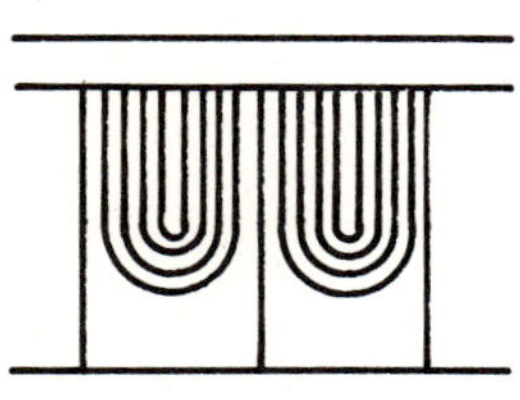

215 Gauze reed

(iii) Ondulé reeds

(*216a, b*) Ondulé or waved effects are produced by distorting the warp or weft. The weft can be distorted by tightening and slackening stripes of warp (the method devised by Peter Collingwood), or an ondulé reed can be used.

A warp ondulé (*a*) has wires arranged fanwise, and a weft ondulé reed (*b*) has undulating baulks at the top and bottom, the wires, otherwise parallel, sloping forwards and backwards at intervals. Both types are deeper than usual, and work by gradually rising and then falling again once in each repeat. Both can be imitated in handweaving by using small sections of reed and sloping or twisting them to beat with.

216 Ondulé reeds

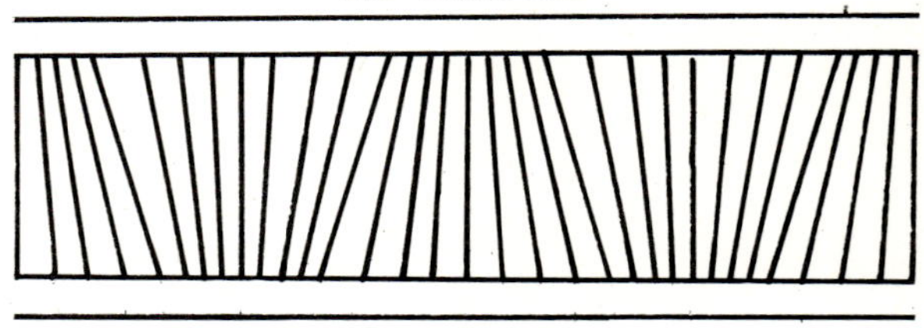

(a) Warp ondulé

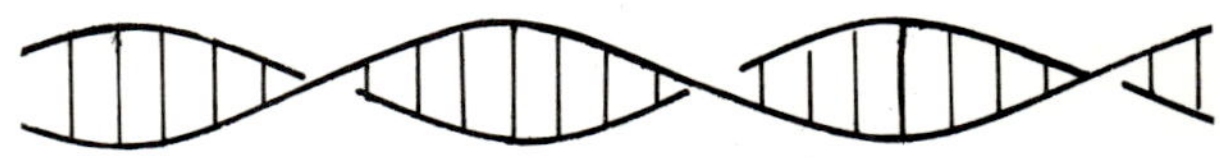

(b) Weft ondulé
(i) plan

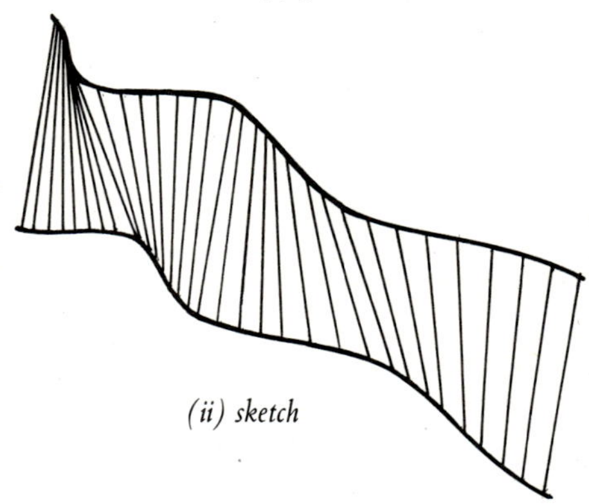

(ii) sketch

Appendix

(*217*) A quick way of weaving samples of several of the basic weaves is to put on a thick cotton warp about 3 yards long and 10 inches wide, with the right half straight threading (1, 2, 3, 4), and the left half waved (1, 2, 3, 4, 3, 2, 1).

The only non-standard liftings are the mock lenos, in which shaft 4 works with shaft 2 throughout, which is then equivalent to threading 1, 2, 3, 2, 3, 2.

On the second part of the warp, colour and weave samples can be woven by staining the warp on the loom. The warp is wound forward till the fell of the cloth is at the breast beam. A shed is opened, e.g. shafts 1 and 3 raised, and a piece of plastic sheet put flat in the shed. The raised part of the warp is dabbed with a sponge soaked in ink, liquid shoe dye, or something similar, and allowed to dry; then it is wound back and woven up. The dye is never fast because of the dressing in the warp and the surface application, so the samples can be only steam pressed to finish them.

wills shaft	Waved or	$\frac{3}{1}$	Straight
	Point	$\frac{2}{2}$	
	Twills	$\frac{1}{3}$	Twills
(ii) *b*	3 and 3 Stitched Hopsack		
(ii) *a*	3 and 3 Hopsack		
(ii) *a*			2 and 2 Hopsack
(i)			Plain Weave

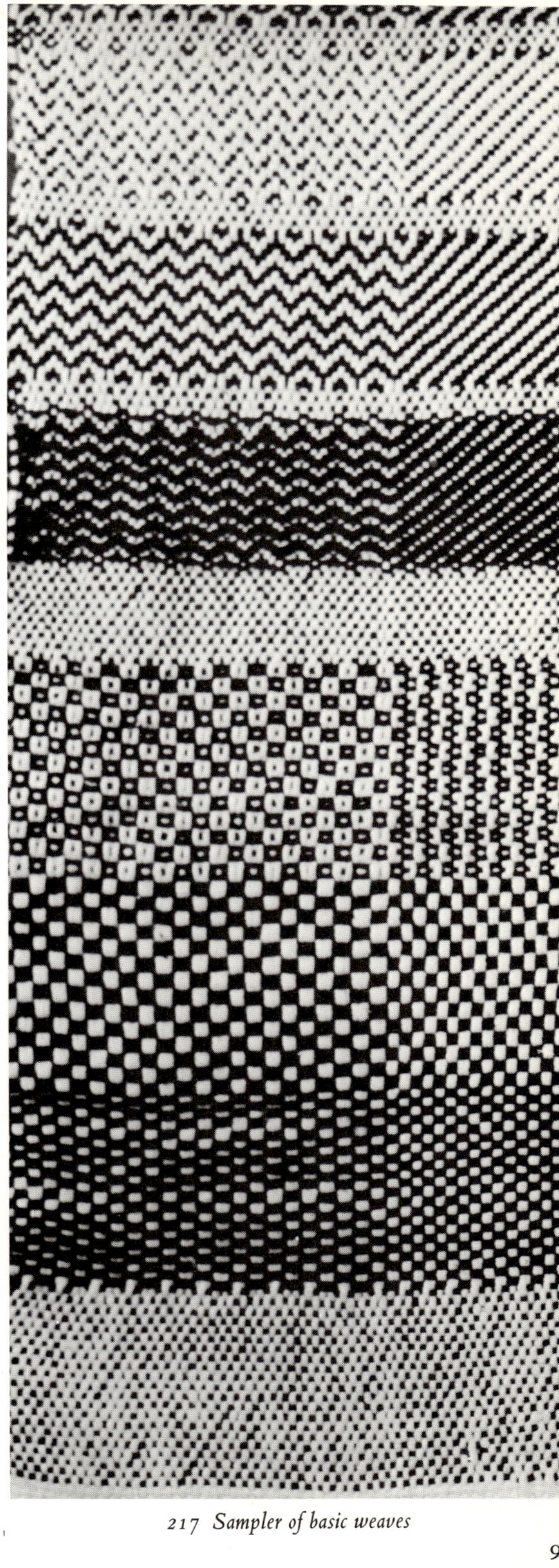

217 Sampler of basic weaves

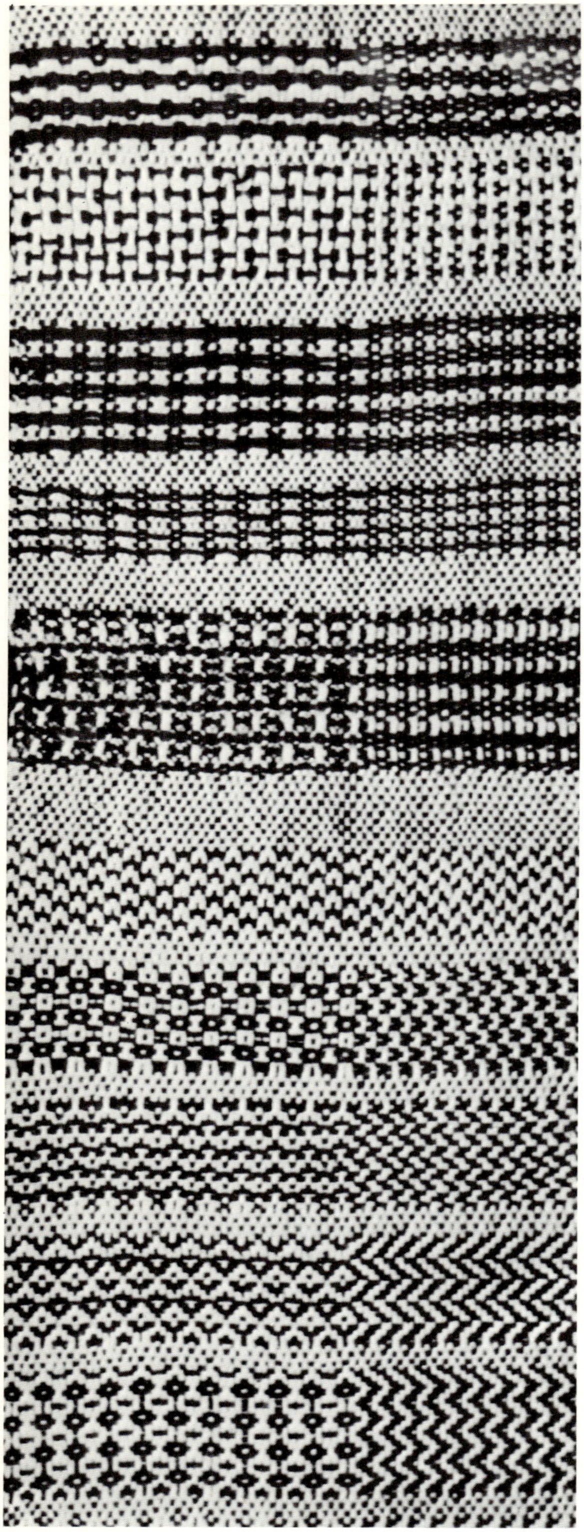

	Half dropped 3 and 1 Mock leno	
6 (i) *b*	3 and 3 Canvas weave	
6 (i) *c*	5 and 1 Mock leno (5 pick)	
	3 and 1 Mock leno (3 pick)	
6 (i) *d*	Honeycomb	
	Warp-way Barley-corn	Warp-way Broken Twill
		Weft-way Barley-corn
		Weft-way Broken Twill
		Weft-way Herringbone
Twills 4-shaft	Diamonds	$\frac{2}{2}$ Waved Twill

Index

The numbers in *italic* refer to the illustrations